Gendered Responses to Male Offending in Barbados

T0347952

It is generally accepted that men commit more crimes than women. The widespread acceptance of this view is based primarily on the number of convictions with most jurisdictions reporting considerably fewer incarcerated women/girls than men/boys. This manuscript argues however that decisions made by the various stakeholders that play a role in the incarceration of men are inherently gendered. These decisions are based on patriarchal perceptions and stereotypes related to the familial roles of men and women, and by extension their motivations for offending. Few studies have sought to explore the nature of these perceptions, and the effect these may have on incarceration patterns. Indeed, this form of inquiry remains absent from the research agenda of Caribbean criminologists. Using qualitative data from Barbados, this book analyses the extent to which these factors are taken into consideration not only by the police and members of the judiciary, but by examining the gendered decisions made by shop managers and proprietors in cases involving shoplifting, it seeks to analyse the extent to which these factors are taken into consideration before incidents reach the justice system. Critically, this book seeks also to juxtapose these assumptions against testimony from men incarcerated at Her Majesty's Prison. The large proportion of males in Caribbean prisons when compared to their female counterparts necessitates an investigation into the factors that may contribute to differential treatment as they move through the justice system. Using data from Barbados, the present study seeks to fill this need.

Corin Bailey is a Senior research Fellow at the Sir Arthur Lewis Institute of Social and Economic Studies at the University of the West Indies, Cave Hill Campus. He is a sociologist with a specific focus on crime and poverty-related research.

Routledge Studies in Crime and Society

Gendered Responses to Male Offending in Barbados
Patriarchal Perceptions and Their Effect on Offender Treatment

Corin Bailey

Routledge
Taylor & Francis Group

LONDON AND NEW YORK

First published 2020
by Routledge
2 Park Square, Milton Park, Abingdon, Oxon OX14 4RN

and by Routledge
605 Third Avenue, New York, NY 10017

First issued in paperback 2022

Routledge is an imprint of the Taylor & Francis Group, an informa business

Copyright © 2020 Corin Bailey

Publisher's Note
The publisher has gone to great lengths to ensure the quality of this reprint but points out that some imperfections in the original copies may be apparent.

British Library Cataloguing-in-Publication Data
A catalogue record for this book is available from the British Library

Library of Congress Cataloging-in-Publication Data
A catalog record has been requested for this book

ISBN: 978-0-367-18341-7 (hbk)
ISBN: 978-0-367-49951-8 (pbk)
ISBN: 978-0-429-06091-5 (ebk)

DOI: 10.4324/9780429060915

Typeset in Times New Roman
by codeMantra

Contents

Abbreviations

CALC	Country Assessments of Living Conditions
CARICOM	Caribbean Community
CBD	Central Business District
CDB	Caribbean Development Bank
CPA	Country Poverty Assessments
GAD	Gender and Development
GST	General Strain Theory
JSIF	Jamaica Social Investment Fund
KMA	Kingston Metropolitan Area
NCVS	National Crime Victimisation Survey
PRA	Participatory Rapid Appraisal
PROTECT	Prosecutorial Remedies and Other Tools to End the Exploitation of Children Today
RBPF	Royal Barbados Police Force
SRA	Sentencing Reform Act
UN	United Nations
UNICEF	United Nations Children's Fund
UNODC	United Nations Office on Drugs and Crime
WICP	The Women in the Caribbean Project

1 Introduction

Crime in Barbados and the Caribbean

As a small island state in the Caribbean, Barbados presents unique perspectives and challenges for research. At the same time, this context offers opportunities for analysis and policy-making that resonate with other countries of the region and around the world that may share commonalities typical of former colonies and plantation economies. The level and changing nature of crime in the Caribbean has led to increasing concern among researchers and policy makers. While during the 1960s property crimes dominated the official statistics, today, the criminal landscape in the region is characterised by violent crime. There is evidence to suggest rates of violent crime in the Caribbean among the highest in the world (UNODC, 2013). Sutton and Ruprah (2017) reported, for example, that the average rate of victimisation and assault in the Caribbean is higher than in any other region globally. High rates have been reported for some of the Leeward Islands, the Dominican Republic, Haiti, Jamaica and the US Virgin Islands. In Jamaica between 1982 and 1997, the homicide rate more than doubled. Between 2003 and 2005 the rate rose from 36 to 58 per 100,000 – among the highest in the world (UNODC; World Bank, 2007).

The high level of violent crime in the region has direct links to the trade in illicit drugs. Drug trafficking through the Caribbean began in the 1970s as South American drug cartels took advantage of the advantageous geographical location of the Caribbean that made it well placed to receive drugs from South America and export to the major markets in the United States and Europe. In addition to the benefits of the geographical location, the trade is also allowed to flourish as a result of failures by successive Caribbean governments to secure coastlines and territorial waters (UNODC; World Bank, 2007). Cocaine and

Marijuana are the two main substances trafficked through the region. The proximity of Trinidad and Tobago to Venezuela has made it a favourable first landing spot for cocaine, after which it is transported to other Caribbean islands in preparation to be moved to North America and Europe. In 2005 the largest narcotics seizure in Trinidad and Tobago's history was 1.75 tons of pure cocaine seized on Monos Island off the coast of Trinidad (Frederick, 2010). Similarly, the islands of the Netherland Antilles have seen sharp increases in seizures in recent years and account for a considerable share of total arrests for cocaine trafficking in the Caribbean (Frederick, 2010; UNODC; World Bank, 2007). While cocaine originates outside of the Caribbean, the production of marijuana is primarily local with Jamaica the leading producer in the region.

Harriott (2000) identified several stages in the development of violent criminal activity in Jamaica. Prominent among these was the search for alternatives to legitimate activity. Residents of poor urban communities found these in the drug trade and in migration, especially to the United States. These two developments served to transform the nature of Jamaican crime as firearms began to flood the country. The market for illegal weapons in the Caribbean has been a major barrier to the achievement of democratic processes, community safety and economic development. One can point to several examples of the instability caused by the widespread availability of firearms in the Caribbean. Moser and Holland (1997) found that participants in their study were unified in their belief that the violence within their communities became worse with the introduction of crack cocaine, since cocaine brought together drugs and guns. Drug trafficking has had similar effects in the smaller islands of the Eastern Caribbean as well. Islands such as St Kitts and Nevis and St Lucia have seen significant increases in violent crime as gangs seek to fortify and protect their turf from rivals (Frederick, 2010).

Homicide rates have therefore been rising rapidly in many Caribbean countries with Barbados a welcomed outlier. Figure 1.1 provides an illustration of the murder rates in selected Caribbean countries between 2000 and 2013 (Bailey, 2016). Barbados continues to compare favourably with countries such as Trinidad and Tobago, Jamaica and the Bahamas.

The homicide rate in Barbados, despite some fluctuation, has remained consistently low and compares favourably to most countries in the region. This is a fact that has been attributed to the relatively low levels of poverty experienced in Barbados as well as the general absence of organised crime, and associations between politics and crime

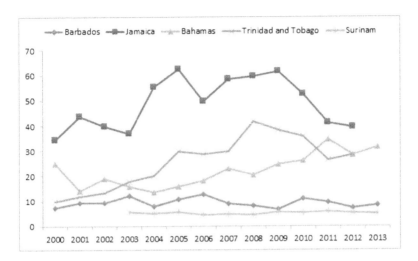

Figure 1.1 Murder rates in selected Caribbean countries, 2000–2013.

that have characterised the criminal landscape of countries such as Jamaica (Ramsay, 2013). Recent increases in the reporting of violent crimes have precipitated national anxiety related to overall crime on the island, particularly considering the country's economic dependence on tourism. In contrast to the level of violent crimes, the rate of property crime remained considerably higher throughout the five-year period 2009–2013, reaching its peak in 2012 (1,758 per 100,000 population) (Bailey, 2016). Similarly, in the Bahamas, rates of property crime have remained considerably higher than violent crimes, although there has been a sharp increase in violent crimes within the past ten years. By contrast, in Jamaica, despite declining rates of violent crimes in recent years, this form of offending continues to dominate national statistics with a ratio of 1.7:1 violent crime to property crime in 2013 (Bailey, 2016).

Few studies have attempted to look beyond official statistics on crime in order to obtain more reliable estimates of overall victimisation. The Barbados Crime Survey (Nuttal, Eversley, Rudder, & Ramsay, 2003) was the first attempt on the island, and revealed very low levels of crime (prevalence rate of 15.4%). In keeping with official statistics, the survey revealed property crimes to be the dominant form of victimisation (prevalence rate of 6.3%). Similar findings emerged from the 2015 Inter-American Development Bank (IDB) victimisation survey, with property crimes again outstripping the incidence of violent offending (Sutton & Ruprah, 2017).

Focus on violent crime

As a result of the general concern for violent crimes therefore, research on crime in the region has focused almost exclusively on the
trends and motivations associated with the perpetration of this form
of criminality, with few studies exploring the circumstances surrounding the occurrence of other forms of offending. Much of the explanations for violent crime have centred around poverty and the associated
conditions that may lead to criminality. Early criminological work in
Jamaica is instructive here. The Report of the Committee on Political
Tribalism (Kerr, 1997) pointed to the cumulative effects of the pro-
tracted period of economic decline during which population growth
had outstripped job creation and in which the education system had
failed to produce young people with the skills to perform in the formal
economy. The National Committee on Crime and Violence (Government of Jamaica, 2002) underscored the loss of independence which
comes with economic hardship, making the poor more likely to commit crime. Levy (1996) too referred to the devouring cycle of poverty
and violence. In the Jamaica Social Investment Fund (JSIF) participatory study of five poor communities in the Kingston Metropolitan
Area (KMA) (Moser & Holland, 1997), participants saw a direct relationship between poverty and violence; interestingly, they did not
perceive their poverty as being solely an income-based phenomenon.
In their view, poverty included some of the broader aspects of deprivation associated with social exclusion such as education. The participants in that study explained that violent robberies outside of the
communities increased when men were out of work and that when opportunities were limited, communities fought against each other over
scarce jobs. More recently, the concept of social exclusion has been
utilised in order to explain how young men, living within the context
of marginalised inner-city communities, characterised by low levels of
educational attainment, high levels of unemployment and a reduction
in the quality of social services and infrastructure turn to violence as
a means of coping with and surviving these conditions (Bailey, 2010).
While for Jamaica, however, a clear association can be identified between rates of homicide and rising inequality, for other islands such as
Trinidad and Tobago and St Lucia, there have been similar increases
in violence without any significant change in inequality. As Kambon
and Henderson (2008) noted, however, these trends may be explained
by the inability of successive governments to arrest the increases in
violent crime that began subsequent to the structural adjustment policies of the 1980s that both countries experienced.

Doing gender in criminology

The nature of crime in the Caribbean, therefore, has helped to shape the research agenda of Caribbean criminology such that it has thus far been characterised primarily by research examining the trends, or motivations for the perpetration of violent crimes. As such, one feature of Caribbean criminology is that relatively little attention has been paid to other forms of offending. A second feature is that despite ground breaking scholarship in Caribbean gender studies (Barriteau, 2001; Leo-Rhynie, 2002; Reddock, 1998), its application to the field of criminology has been somewhat inequitable. One aspect of this neglect is the fact that women's involvement in crime has been largely ignored. Reports from Britain have animated the issue because of the increase in the proportion of women prisoners in British jails who were from the Caribbean and specifically Jamaica (Ford, 2003). Most were imprisoned for drug offenses. They were typically poor, single mothers from deprived urban and rural neighbourhoods, the majority having no previous criminal record or knowledge of the consequences. They were prime targets for male drug dealers who exploited their poverty and their fear of the consequences of non-compliance (Editorial, 2002). Researchers' neglect of the study of women and the justice system in the Caribbean is quite likely a result of the low numbers involved in the system. In Jamaica there are just over 300 women in prison, less than 8 per cent of the prison population (Clarke & Henry-Lee, 2005). In Barbados the number is even smaller with an average female prison population of 33 (Bailey, 2016). Interrogating gender in criminology however is not simply a recognition that women are involved in offending. Another aspect of the neglect, therefore, is that even among explanations for male offending, there have been few attempts at addressing the role that gender plays in various outcomes, such as offender perpetration and punishment. This is the focus of this manuscript.

Western societies have developed a propensity to view men and women as fundamentally different purely as a result of their biological differences. What has come to be viewed as either masculine or feminine has in large part been determined by the fact that men are men, and women are women. Although the notion of sex-linked behaviours still persists, sociological scholarship has in many ways sought to challenge these views. Sex role or gender role theory was integral to an articulation of the fundamental flaw in the manner in which characteristics and roles were automatically assigned to individuals based on their sex. A precursor to the focus on specific roles such as sex and gender was the emergence of role theory with 'role' seen as a concept integral to the social sciences as it provided a critical link between the individual and the social environment (Biddle, 1979; Goffman, 1959). Central to role theory, which began as a theatrical metaphor, was the notion that human behaviour varied from person to person, depending on one's social environment and influences. Three concepts encapsulated the theory: (1) patterned and characteristic social behaviours, (2) identities that are assumed by individuals and (3) expected behaviour that is generally accepted by all parties. Despite some disagreement among role theorists related to terminology and definitions, it is generally agreed that roles are primarily governed by expectations, and that these expectations are cultivated through one's socialisation experiences (BIddle, 1986). Role expectations, therefore, develop and spread through mutual acceptance among a population resulting in cultural norms. There is scholarship within role theory (Parsons & Bales, 1955) that provided analysis of male and female roles within a marriage, referring to these as either task oriented (instrumental) in the case of men, or socioemotional (expressive) in the case of women (Eagly & Wood, 2011). Out of this tradition emerged gender or sex role theory – the analysis of male and female behaviour, or, more specifically, the influence of social structure and culture on behaviour and related expectations (Biddle, 1986).

Gender roles encompass a variety of practices and activities not limited to childhood chores, disparities in status, household labour as well as various employment tasks. Women are traditionally associated with domestic roles, while men assume roles linked with their status as 'breadwinner'. At the root of debate on the subject lies the dichotomy between two competing viewpoints. Those that purport that roles are fixed (entity theory) maintain that there is an intrinsic link between these roles and one's sex. It requires the belief that all characteristics are both biological and unchangeable and results in gender stereotyping (Coleman & Hong, 2008). When applied to the home, therefore, a man may assume temporary responsibility for domestic tasks, but they nevertheless remain intrinsically the domain of women. This is in contrast to incremental theory which suggests that these roles may be interchangeable based on the circumstance (Kray, Howland, Russell, & Jackman, 2016).

Gender role theorists have challenged the notion of unchangeable roles, and have emphasised the belief that these roles are the result of historical assignment, rather than being biologically determined (Eagly, Wood, & Diekman, 2000). Hughes (1945) referred to gender roles as a dynamic process of 'situated identities' in which individuals have the ability to adopt or shed roles depending on the situation, rather than 'master identities' such as sex categorisation. West and Zimmerman (1987) argued that gender does not constitute a set of traits, or roles, but that this notion is allowed to flourish due to its perpetuation by human action. This ongoing activity that influences the day-to-day interactions between individuals they referred to as 'doing gender'. The theorising of gender as a situated action, in addition to dispelling the view that biological differences between men and women govern gender, moves the discussion beyond the problematic portrayal of men and woman as passive actors. It recognises the agency of individuals within the context of structural inequalities such as race, age or gender (Miller J., 2002).

In this sense then, crime and criminology too are gendered in that variables such as perpetration, victimisation, and sentencing/punishment can all reproduce and perpetuate masculine and/or feminine stereotypes and assumptions. The concept of situated action has been used by feminist criminologists to explain the gendered nature of crime primarily as it relates to masculinities whereby crime is a function of men's desire to display masculinity within specific contexts (Simpson & Elis, 1995). The work of Messerschmidt (1993) has been particularly useful in explaining the link between masculinity and street crime. Messerschmidt's doing masculinity incorporated a structured action framework, in which masculinity interacted with issues such as race, class, age and sexuality, in a struggle for social power. Within this context, street crime is a means of obtaining this power (Messerschmidt, 1993). Mullins (2006) provided a particularly useful analysis of the role played by the subordination of less dominant forms of masculinities as well as certain femininities in the culture of street crime. Certain masculinities are viewed as threats to the dominant forms in specific situations, and must be addressed through the use of physical violence, sometimes resulting in the death of one or more of those involved. Similar conclusions were drawn by Baird (2012) in his study of gang violence.

The role of masculinity in the perpetration of violence against women too has been a subject of considerable interest. Scully and Marolla (1985) found that among their sample of convicted rapists, women were viewed as a conquest and affirmation of their masculinity. Indeed, male-perpetrated physical and sexual violence against women has been argued to be the result of a desire to prove one's masculinity to himself, his peers and to his victim (DeKeseredy & Schwartz, 2005). The rape of men by men too is interpreted in similar terms by both victims and perpetrators. It is important to note that rape is not gendered because it is perpetrated by a higher proportion of men than women.

Rather, it is gendered because as a social practice, it perpetuates assumptions related to masculinity (Britton, 2011).

Social institutions too can be gendered in their operation. Britton (2011) made reference to the United States Prison Reform which decided that such was the nature of female criminals that they should be housed in separate units where they would be trained in domestic tasks, such as ironing and starching. Upon parole, they were assigned as domestic workers for the middle class. Although these formalised practices have been discarded for the most part, the prevailing assumptions still exist today with women more likely to be offered classes in cosmetology while men are more likely to be sentenced to hard labour or military style discipline (Britton, 2003). Similarly, offenders can experience a gendered interaction with the justice system by way of the intricacies that surround arrests and convictions. It is well established that in general, official statistics are seen as unreliable as crime rates often do not provide an accurate representation of criminal behaviour (Kelly, Lovett, & Regan, 2005). This problem assumes greater significance when comparing male and female rates of criminal involvement. The relatively large number of men incarcerated when compared to women can be potentially misleading, and not truly representative of the disparity in offending levels since many researchers believe that official figures are particularly unreflective of the extent of women's involvement. One of the reasons put forward for this is the notion that there is a bias towards women within the justice system (Demuth & Steffensmeier, 2004; Spohn & Belchner, 2000; Steffensmeier & Demuth, 2006). It is argued that the disparity between the offending levels of men and women is not as large as statistics suggest, since men experience harsher treatment than women when they come in contact with the justice system. Some argue that this situation is changing somewhat, and in many developed countries, an increasing number of girls and women are being convicted for serious offenses, with the number increasing at a more rapid rate than that of men. Despite these increases, however, recent studies have found that gender disparity in sentencing still exists with women receiving more lenient treatment from the courts than men (Curry, Lee, & Rodriguez, 2004).

The present study

It is true that when considering socially constructed identities, it is important to recognise that these rarely operate in isolation from one another. This was a theme explored by Stuart Hall in his theorisings about race and ethnicity. Hall rejected the notion that race was a purely ideological or cultural concept, and instead maintained that it was evident in every aspect of human interaction. As such, he believed that race could only be adequately understood within the context of, in particular, social and economic relations (Hall, 2002).

The work of Kimberle Crenshaw explored the manner in which gender interacts with other concepts such as race and class. Crenshaw (1989) referred to this as intersectionality. In critiquing US antidiscrimination legislation, and in examining the employment experiences of black women, she argued that the racism faced by black women is unique, and as such should not be treated as if part of a homogenous experience. She concluded that many of these experiences cannot be analysed within the traditional contexts of race and gender discrimination. Similarly, Crenshaw's engagement with race and gender was evident in her analysis of what she labelled as structural intersectionality – the manner in which for black women, the combination of race and gender resulted in distinctly unique experiences of rape and domestic violence when compared to white women. Within the context of battered women's shelters in Los Angeles, Crenshaw found that the poverty experienced by most of the women meant that administrators had to address not only their physical victimisation but also the combination of oppressive factors that reduced their alternatives to their abusive relationships (Crenshaw, 1991). Indeed, the poverty faced by many black women is exacerbated by child care responsibilities, and, in turn, compounded by racial and class oppression. As such, Crenshaw believed that these experiences required intervention strategies that took these unique circumstances into consideration. This was a similar theme explored by Ritchie (1996) in explaining how the intersection of race, gender and poverty resulted in the propulsion of women in criminal activity.

Intersectionality deems as inaccurate therefore, the notion that different social interactions and identities are mutually exclusive but, instead, blend together to produce unique experiences for different groups (Brown & Misra, 2003). Collins (2000) captured the complexity of the concept in his reference to a 'matrix of domination' rather than a set of social structures that can be analysed individually. A recognition of this complexity is critical to reversing the power and privilege imbalance within academic discourse and if ignored will continue to, for example, fail to account for the many levels of victimisation experienced by black women (Sigle-Rushton & Lindstrom, 2013). The result is theories that are applicable only to select groups.

Intersectionality has made a critical contribution to feminist scholarship through its focus on inclusion, privilege and power and the manner in which it encourages the questioning of existing assumptions.

It is a concept that has been used exclusively to address the interests of women. It has been suggested, however, that there is a reluctance to treat men as gendered subjects as well (Hearn & Collinson, 2006). Murray (2015) argued that the prevailing view that men assume the role of victor over women in all circumstances was an erroneous one since there are instances in which gender roles and stereotypes do not operate to men's advantage, even if those same roles offer them positions of power. This manuscript provides analysis of instances in which patriarchy and existing gender stereotypes operate to the disadvantage of men. While not applying the theory of intersectionality directly, I believe that the concept is useful to serve as a background against which to frame the notion that poverty and gender may be interacting to shape men's experiences with the Barbadian justice system.

It is generally accepted that men commit more crimes than women. The widespread acceptance of this view is based primarily on the number of convictions. In Britain women account for only 4.6 per cent of the total prison population. In the United States that figure is 9.8 per cent while in Jamaica and Barbados women account for 4.7 and 3.6 per cent, respectively (Walmsley, 2017). This manuscript argues, however, that decisions made by the various stakeholders that play a role in the incarceration of men are therefore inherently gendered. Few studies have sought to explore the nature of these perceptions, and the effect these may have on incarceration patterns. Indeed, this form of inquiry remains absent from the research agenda of Caribbean criminologists. Using qualitative data from Barbados, this manuscript analyses the extent to which these factors are taken into consideration not only by the police and members of the judiciary, but by examining the gendered decisions made by shop managers and proprietors in cases involving shoplifting, it seeks to analyse the extent to which these factors are taken into consideration before incidents reach the justice system. The large proportion of males in Caribbean prisons when compared to their female counterparts necessitates an investigation into the factors that may contribute to differential treatment as they move through the justice system. Using data from Barbados, the present study seeks to fill this need. Specifically, the following questions are explored:

1   What is the nature of the perceptions held by civil society, the police and the judiciary, as it relates to male and female roles within the family in the context of child rearing?
2   What is the nature of the perceptions held by civil society, the police and the judiciary, as it relates to male and female motivations to offend?

3   How do these perceptions affect the treatment of male offenders as they come into contact with civil society, the police and the justice system, as they make their way through the various stages of the justice system?
4   What are the motivations to offend, among male offenders incarcerated for drug smuggling in Barbados?

Methodology

Research for this manuscript focused on two forms of offending. The crime of shoplifting was chosen as it provided a perfect opportunity to examine the interaction between civil society and offenders in Barbados. In addition, drug smuggling was chosen because it represented a non-violent crime for which a large proportion of non-Barbadian offenders were incarcerated. Engaging with these offenders therefore allowed for insight to be obtained related to the motivating factors of men from across the Caribbean.

In order to achieve the desired aims of the study, and to generate rich insights into perceptions that may influence the treatment of male offenders, a qualitative methodology was utilised, with three methods of data collection and analysis employed. Semi-structured interviews have long been used as a means of capturing data in criminological research and thus were employed in the present study to explore the origin and current nature of perceptions on gender roles and motivating factors, and the manner in which these may affect decisions as they relate to incarceration rates. Interviews were held with shop owners/managers in the Central Business District (CBD) of the city of Bridgetown, Barbados[1]; Magistrates that would generally preside over cases of shoplifting and/or drug smuggling[2]; and men and women incarcerated for drug smuggling at Her Majesty's Prison.[3] In addition, focus groups were held with male and female members of the Royal Barbados Police Force.[4] Finally, courtroom observation was employed in order to assess the manner in which male offenders were treated by local magistrates.

In Chapter 2 I draw upon reviews of current critical thinking in the area of gendered treatment of offenders in order to develop a comprehensive conceptual framework of the causes and consequences.

In Chapter 3 I provide the detailed background on gender and family relations in Barbados and the Caribbean, against which many of the stakeholders that come into contact with offenders were raised.

In Chapter 4 I examine relations between male offenders and civil society in the form of shop owners/managers, as well as interactions between male offenders and the police.

In Chapter 5 I analyse the treatment of male offenders by the courts. I draw upon testimony from Magistrates that would generally preside over cases of shoplifting and/or drug smuggling, as well as Courtroom observation.

In light of the testimonies provided in previous chapters, in Chapter 6 I shift the discussion towards the voices of offenders themselves, who offer insight into the factors that precipitated their own involvement in crime.

In Chapter 7 I conclude and synthesise the main findings of the study and discuss key themes to have emerged from the data.

Notes

1 Twenty interviews with shop owners/proprietors from a sample of retails stores in the CBD of the city of Bridgetown in Barbados. Respondents were asked questions related to their experiences with shoplifting; the manner in which they deal with incidents of shoplifting perpetrated by both male and female offenders; their opinions on male and female roles.
2 Semi-structured interviews with nine (of a total of 11) magistrates. The Magistrate Courts have jurisdiction over civil, family and criminal matters and operate within eight judicial districts.
3 Semi-structured interviews with 11 male inmates.
4 Focus group sessions with members of the Royal Barbados Police Force. Separate sessions were held with men and women officers who would typically respond to the types of offenses relevant to this study.

2 Concepts and context

Gendered treatment of offenders

Much of the work on the gendered treatment of offenders by the justice system has examined the manner in which male offenders have been treated in relation to their female criminal counterparts. These, for the most part, have concluded that men are in fact treated more harshly. The first stage at which an offender comes into contact with the justice system is the arrest stage and so a lot of attention has been paid to the circumstances surrounding this interaction. Krohn, Curry and Nelson-Kilger (1983) in investigating the treatment of offenders in the arrest stage found that there was a distinct propensity for men to experience harsh treatment when compared to women. They were consistently more likely to be arrested (Wright, 1993) as long as women displayed appropriate gender behaviour and characteristics. Wilczynski (1997) found that the criminal justice system saw men as bad and normal and so treated them accordingly. In contrast they saw female offenders as abnormal and in need of more delicate treatment. Stolzenberg and D'Alessio (2004) used data from the National Incident-Based Reporting System in order to look at the effect of gender on the likelihood of arrest for 555,752 incidents of kidnapping, forcible rape, forcible fondling, robbery, aggravated assault, simple assault and intimidation in 19 states in the District of Columbia during 2000. The data allowed them to determine the likelihood of arrest for males and females based on sex-specific offending, using reports from victims of these crimes. They found that men were considerably more likely to be arrested for the majority of the crimes, particularly for kidnapping and forcible fondling. Overall, they argued that the disparity was in large part due to the leniency afforded to girls and women by the justice system.

Nagel and Weitzman (1971) examined the sentencing decisions for men and women charged with grand larceny and assault. They found that men were more likely to be sent to prison than women, who typically received suspended sentences or probation. Nagel and Hagan (1983) demonstrated that women were given lighter sentences except in high severity offences. Simon (1975) too concluded that women were given preferential treatment in the courtroom. Many of these early studies were criticised for their failure to account for the seriousness of the offenses, prior offending and for their narrow focus on sentencing patterns. When Moulds (1978) controlled for the gravity of the offense and for previous convictions, however, the outcome was substantially the same. More recently, Rogers and Davies (2007) utilised mock jurors to examine reactions to sexual assault and concluded that jurors perceived males as more culpable than female defendants.

It is true that not all studies have found the justice system to favour women however. Visher (1983) in an attempt to include those who had been filtered out at an earlier stage analysed arrest decisions and found that there were occasions when women did not in fact benefit from preferred treatment. Those women who displayed behaviour considered appropriate for their sex were treated leniently, while those who departed from the gender stereotype enjoyed no advantage. There are situational factors, such as the presence of bystanders, which come into play when boys and men were apprehended, but not in the case of girls and women. Despite some opposition, however, the notion that male offenders receive harsher treatment in comparison to women and girls is one of the more consistent findings within criminological literature that focuses on court outcomes. Indeed, these findings have typically transcended both time and location.

These findings have precipitated a large body of research aimed at examining the manner and context within which this disparity in treatment takes place. There are two basic and competing approaches for understanding the treatment of offenders. Formal rationality argues that any variation in sentencing is the result of appropriate legal considerations such as the offense committed or part criminal record (Dixon, 1995; Ulmer, 1997), while bounded rationality suggests that extra-legal considerations play a significant role. These include expectations and biases such as race, class and gender. It is within the context of bounded rationality that two theoretical perspectives have emerged as particularly influential. The chivalry thesis emerged in the 1950s and is based on societal assumptions and cultural stereotypes concerning gender. Second, there is familial paternalism, which takes into consideration the impact of the parental role of female offenders in particular. It is important to note here that these theories have received minimal consideration within the Caribbean context.

Chivalry and the justice system

The term 'chivalry' originated in tenth-century Medieval Europe, re-lated to the institution of Knighthood and was associated with ideals of knightly virtues, honour and courtly love. The knights possessed an array of enviable characteristics – military training, a war-horse and military equipment, all which afforded them a large amount of wealth and prestige. After the twelfth century, the world chivalry became associated with notions of moral, religious and social codes of knightly conduct. It came to refer to the manners that were pos-sessed by the knight which he displayed both at home in his castle and with his court. Women were special beneficiaries of the chivalry of the knight and among his duties was what was often referred to as 'courtly' love. A knight was to serve his lady, and after her, all other ladies. Implicit in these duties was a general gentleness and gracious-ness to all women. Though chivalry as an institution has long since disappeared, it is argued that the associated 'reverence' for woman has for the most part remained, with practices of chivalry continuing to be a large part of accepted social codes. This is the legacy of the era of chivalry (Moulds, 1978).

Chivalry, when applied to the justice system, has often been used in conjunction with the term 'paternalism', a concept that has its roots in a type of behaviour that is associated with the treatment of a daughter by her father. Three basic premises of paternalism exist: a child is ignorant, and as such, can be deceived and manipulated to serve the needs of his/her parent; a child is not fully aware of his/her role and so is in need of guidance; and a child is defenceless and in need of protection (Pitt-Rivers, 1968). Moulds (1978) argued that the inevitable effect in a society that has been allowed to absorb these beliefs is that the actions of those who affect the law either directly or indirectly become inconsistent with the operation of a demo-cratic state. This is what he referred to as ". . . a basic denial of self-determination" (p. 419).

Writing in 1901, Frances Keller was one of the first to theorise this notion of chivalry as it applies to the justice system. He argued that chivalrous attitudes account for much of the discrepancy found in of-ficial statistics.

> Women are less vigorously prosecuted than men. When indicted, judgments are obtained with greater difficulty and their punish-ment is less severe. A study of municipal court records reveals clearly the difference in penalties for the same offenses committed

by both sexes. This is due partly to sympathy and to consideration shown by officers, judges, juries, attorneys and others who administer criminal laws.

(Kellor, 1901, p. 159)

Morrison (1902) echoed the views of Keller, arguing that though he was not saying that women committed more crimes than men, that the difference was 'overestimated' because of the preferential treatment that was afforded to them by society. He said that not only is a woman faced with the same level of evidence less likely than a man to be convicted, but also members of the public are less inclined to press charges against them. He said that the result of this was a misrepresentation of the level of female criminal participation in official statistics (Morrison, 1902).

Following on from these writings, one of the most influential proponents of the chivalry theory was Otto Pollack. He explained:

> One of the outstanding concomitants of the existing inequality between the sexes is chivalry and the general protective attitude of the man toward woman. This attitude exists on the part of the male victim of crime as well as on the part of the officers of the law, who are still largely male in our society. Men hate to accuse women. . .Police officers dislike to arrest them, district attorneys to prosecute them, Judges and Juries to find them guilty.

(Pollack, 1950, p. 151)

The views of Pollack and others greatly influenced the direction of research undertaken from the 1970s, and precipitated considerable scholarship, aimed at investigating whether or not chivalry played a major role within the justice system. Scholars have tested the hypothesis by way of examinations of the sentencing outcomes for men and women that come before the courts for the same crime (Moulds, 1978). Others have observed the treatment of male and female offenders by officials of the court with many concluding that women are in fact enjoying some comparative leniency in sentencing (Steffensmeier, Kramer, & Streifel, 1993; Steffensmeier & Montivans, 2000). Studies examining media portrayals of female criminals have offered support to the belief that chivalrous attitudes held by members of the judiciary are manifestations of broader societal views. Weimann and Fishman (1988) found that within the media, women tend to be portrayed as reluctant offenders, driven by circumstance or male manipulation, rather than the greed, revenge or substance abuse generally assigned to men. This has the inevitable effect of reducing societal empathy for male offenders.

There has however been much disagreement over these conclusions. Notions of chivalry in the justice system have received substantial criticism with opponents arguing that these ideas, particularly early aspects which painted a picture of women as 'evil', stem from sexist ideologies. It has been suggested that the justice system is, in reality, more than prepared to give harsher penalties to women who do not act in accordance with traditional feminine roles (Horowitz & Pottieger, 1991). Others have pointed towards the 'inconclusive' nature of the results of such investigations. Morris (1987) argued that the evidence did not prove that sexual discrimination occurred in the criminal justice system. She felt more so, that to infer chivalry was to not fully comprehend the complex nature of the sentencing of both male and female offenders.

Familial-based justice

Moulds (1978) noted the need for a distinction to be made between the concepts of chivalry and judicial paternalism. While chivalry is rooted in a superficial deference to women, judicial paternalism focuses on the social and legal inferiority suffered by women, the result of which is the belief among a male-dominated justice system that women need to be supported and/or protected. Daly (1987) suggested that this 'conceptual confusion' leading to the concepts being used interchangeably was due to an erroneous assumption that the leniency that appeared to be afforded to women automatically meant that the target of the judicial protection was the women themselves. Indeed, there is the notion that, paramount in the minds of those that interact with offenders as they come into contact with the law, is a concern not for the protection of women, but the protection of families, and specifically children. Kruttschnitt's (1982) theory of informal social control is one of a number of attempts to explain how ties to families can affect incarceration. Because social controls have been shown to reduce the propensity to reoffend, it follows therefore in the eyes of state actors that the greater the social control upon an offender, the more worthy they are of lenient treatment. The level of dependence one has on family members therefore, is of particular relevance since social controls increase the more 'tied' one is to others. Kruttschnitt believed that informal social control was less significant in the lives of men, as a result of the lesser likelihood that they would be economically dependent on others. Daly believed that while the work of Kruttschnitt was useful, it was not adequate in explaining gender disparities in treatment since women, in addition to being more likely to be dependent on others, were also more likely than men to be the ones on whom others were dependent (Daly, 1987). In an articulation of what she termed familial paternalism, Daly argued that decision makers were faced with 'practical considerations' associated with the incarceration of offenders with dependent children. By combining Kruttschnitt's social control with her notion of practical considerations, Daly concluded that familied offenders were seen as more anchored in the normative social order because their day-to-day lives are restricted by having family responsibilities. There is a reluctance therefore to punish children, by incarcerating the person on whom they depend. Daly's conclusions were based on qualitative interviews conducted with judges who spoke about the negative consequences of removing the main provider for children, from their homes. Judges were primarily concerned therefore not simply with the fact that an offender may have children, but with the specific role played in the children's lives.

Contemporary scholarship on the impact of familial paternalism on incarceration has supported a positive association. Freiburger (2010) in examining the effect of offender family status on judges' decision making found that the 'emotional support' provided for children was pivotal, and thus those providing this form of support were less likely to be incarcerated than those who were not. Financial support alone was not enough to protect against incarceration. In a subsequent study Freiburger (2011) assessed the effect of familied status on drug offenders living in Allegheny County, Pennsylvania and concluded that living with a child reduced the odds of incarceration by 48 per cent. In offering leniency towards offenders that play integral roles in children's lives, decision makers are attempting to achieve equilibrium between punishing the guilty (the offender) and protecting the innocent (children). To this end therefore, they are reluctant to separate caregivers from their dependents.

Familial paternalism is predicated therefore on the notion that any disparity in the treatment of offenders is based not on gender, but on the different family roles played by offenders. If this is the case, however, it should follow that if it is deemed detrimental to the welfare of children to remove familied women from the home, the same should be true for the removal of familied men. Research has found that, indeed, familied men are less likely to be incarcerated than non-familied men. Daly's (1987) examination of New York City criminal court decisions revealed that male and female offenders with no children had the same likelihood of incarceration. In addition, single men with children were more likely to be afforded leniency than single men without children. When comparing familied men and women, however, there was sentencing disparity, a circumstance which Daly argued was the result of the courts attaching a higher social cost to the incarceration of women than men. Among familied men and women, the court officials see more 'good' mothers than 'good' fathers. Gender divisions in work and family life make the removal of women, who are deemed more likely to play a caring role, more detrimental in the eyes of court officials than the removal of men. Caregiving labour is more indispensable to the family than the economic support that is typically assumed by the male. What matters most is the day-to-day care, a conclusion supported by Simon and Ahn-Redding (2005). It is important to reiterate here that these decisions take root in the prevailing assumption among the judiciary that crucial familial responsibilities are more likely to be provided by women, and so as a result, by comparison, there is less reluctance to incarcerate men. This does not however mean that familied women benefit in all circumstances, a fact illustrated by Bickle and Peterson (1991) who demonstrated that even among women, simply being a parent was not good enough. It was important to be viewed as a good mother in order to be afforded lenient treatment. Decisions were being made within the courts based on assumptions about family dynamics. In confirming the privileging of the good mother, Daly and Bordt (1995) acknowledged the manner in which culture and social institutions influence the justice system's recognition of gender differences.

The impact of these assumptions on rates of incarceration has even greater significance when one takes into consideration the fact that stereotypes related to the family roles of men and women are held not only by agents of the state, but by members of the wider society as well. This means that in certain circumstances, there are opportunities for filtering out offenders even before the arrest stage. This manuscript argues that within Barbados, the assumptions and stereotypes that govern familial paternalism are the function of patriarchal gender relations.

Patriarchal gender relations

Human interactions are, to a large extent, guided by behavioural expectations. There are manners in which men and women are expected to behave, or roles they are expected to assume, based on local social and cultural norms, with these norms being passed down from generation to generation. Within patriarchal systems, the roles that are ascribed to men and boys assume a greater level of significance than those ascribed to women and girls. Patriarchy is a social construct therefore, which positions men (the patriarchs) as superior to women. It refers to a historical system created as a result of changes in demographic, ecological, historical and cultural features of society from which has emerged ". . . social structures and practices in which men dominate, oppress and exploit women" (Walby, 1990, p. 20).

The origins of patriarchy can be traced back to the early beginnings of civilisation when due to maternal responsibilities such as child birth and child care, women were unable to take part in hunting activities. Men therefore became associated with providing a role that was seen as dominant in comparison to the more domestic roles assumed by women. As civilisation developed these notions intensified with men assuming a central position in social, economic and political life while women were relegated to the periphery (Verma Singh, 2016).

Millet (1969) was one of the first to introduce the concept of patriarchy into academic scholarship. She argued for the existence of two main principles that underpin the concept – (1) that males dominate females and (2) that older males dominate younger males. These values are perpetuated primarily within the family, as this is the chief institution that socialises individuals by way of social constructs of stereotypical roles of masculinity and femininity that are internalised. If society is the macro level patriarchal unit, then, operating at the micro level, encouraging individuals to conform to society's norms and expectations is the family. According to Millet, classic patriarchy assigns ownership of wife and child to the father who is the head of the household and thus assumes control of a women's mobility, sexuality and labour. The main function of the family within this system therefore is the socialisation of the young. Although these ideologies are cultivated within the family they are perpetuated and legitimised by external institutions such as the school, media and church (Desai & Krishnaraj, 2004). Most religions, for example, endorse patriarchy both through their teachings, as well as through the organisation of roles within the church administrative hierarchy.

The issue of gender roles assumes particular significance as it relates to this manuscript. In all societies, biological differences have been used as a means of justifying the assigning of specific roles to men and women. Post-modernist feminist thought has been instrumental, however, in not only critiquing these unfair norms but also dispelling the notion that femininity and masculinity are inherent. Feminist scholarship argues that women are socialised into certain roles because this suits the interests of men. Patriarchy oversees the indoctrination of women into the narrow identity confines of mother, daughter and wife (Verma Singh, 2016). Women have, to a large extent, been characterised as a homogenous group with social, political and psychological qualities that are separate and distinct from their male counterparts and as such render them more suitable for specific roles. In reality however, there is an intimate relationship between one's gender identity, the associated roles people gravitate towards, and the influence that society's social structures have had on them. Those with dominant characteristics tend to orient themselves with traditionally dominant roles while the less dominant gravitate towards subordinate roles. That women often align themselves (or are aligned) with the latter is the direct result of a patriarchal system (Sundberg, 2004).

Even more important than biology therefore are the socially and culturally constructed beliefs that are handed down from generation to generation (Gilmore, 1990; Verma Singh, 2016). As mentioned earlier, families play a significant role in this process since from birth, boys and girls are taught accepted manners of behaviour. Gender socialisation therefore instructs individuals on what is expected behaviour for both sexes. The formation of individual and collective gender identities is critical to who we are, and how we react to others. Traditional gender roles determine what society views as feminine or masculine. In order to be feminine therefore, a woman must display personality characteristics that society views as befitting. Similarly, in any given society, there are approved ways of being an adult male. Boys learn that maleness requires them to be dominating and that the critical role within the family is that of provider (Gilmore, 1990; Lerner, 1986). Indeed, Hooks (2004) described her childhood socialisation experience as one in which she was encouraged to be nurturing, weak and submissive, while her brother was taught to be the provider, strong, and to reject the notion that it should be his responsibility to nurture others.

Hooks argued that both men and women participate in this 'tortured value system' whereby half of our natural traits (those deemed masculine) enjoy a higher status than the other half (those deemed feminine). The result of this is that within patriarchal societies, not only is there the tendency for men and women to gravitate towards those roles that have been culturally assigned, but there is also the expectation among both sexes that this is the norm. This manuscript argues that it is these patriarchal expectations that govern assumptions made by various stakeholders, as to the gendered motivations of male criminal offenders in Barbados.

Gendered motivations for offending

Traditional explanations for criminality emerged in the late nineteenth century and focused primarily on male motivations for offending. Scholars at the time based their views on the notion that innate individual characteristics were in large part responsible for criminal actions (Freud, 1933; Lombroso & Ferrero, 1958; Thomas, 1923). The positivist writings of Cesare Lombroso, widely believed to be the 'father' of criminology, for example, focused on the physical and psychological characteristics of offenders arguing that the criminal was in fact a separate species with distinct features such as large jaws, high cheek bones, extra toes, nipples or fingers as well as other identifying characteristics such as insensitivity to pain. In studying the causes of crime, Lombroso also suggested a racial hierarchy in which black Africans were at the bottom, and white Europeans at the top (Lombroso & Ferrero, 1958). By focusing exclusively on the physical and psychological characteristics of offenders, proponents of this positivist ideology effectively ignored the effect of other possible causes such as socialisation.

The theoretical shift towards the importance of structural factors such as economic deprivation in explaining criminal involvement is particularly well illustrated by the work of the Chicago School. Robert Merton's theory of strain, heavily influenced by Durkheim's anomie for example, posited that frustration arose when everyone in society accepted similar goals, but not all had the means to legitimately achieve them. Opportunities to realise these goals were unequal, and as a result rules were abandoned leading to a state of anomie or normlessness, which, in turn, produced strain or pressure on individuals to respond (Merton, 1949). Merton argued that this strain was primarily economic and appeared to apply only to men. Americans place great value on high achievement and success, and everyone is encouraged to be competitive and to reach for success. Unfortunately, Merton argued, too little emphasis is placed upon the utilisation of approved means to achieve success. The disadvantaged in the society have internalised mainstream success goals, but are denied the educational and occupational means of achieving them. The response of individuals is shaped by their position in the social structure, and the poor are likely to innovate by turning to crime. Cohen (1955) applied the strain theory specifically to adolescent working-class males. Frustrated by their lack of success, these boys rejected the goals of mainstream society in favour of a delinquent subculture where a high value was placed on success in breaking the law. Cohen believed that as opposed to girls, whose only significant strain was to 'marry well', boys suffered the significant economic stress of employment and income in their lives.

Other efforts at explaining criminality sought to move beyond the notion that economic hardship was the primary motivation to offend. General strain theory (GST) is credited with a revision of traditional strain. Agnew (1985) argued that negative events create pressures for delinquency. Rather than focusing only on financial pressures, he included a number of sources of psychological strain, which may lead to delinquency as well. Similarly, Edwin Sutherland's differential association refuted the notion that poverty was the major cause of crime among males. He argued instead that criminal behaviour was learned and as a result was heavily linked to one's peer group association (Sutherland, 1939).

In Chapter 1 I noted that a recognition of the role of gender in shaping the experiences and behaviour of boys and men came in the form of Messerschmidt's focus on structured action and gendered crime (Messerschmidt, 1993). Masculinity theory argues that it is essential for men to confirm their manhood through activities and practices that assert their maleness. It is the approved way of being male in any given society (Condry & Condry, 1976; Giddens, 1993; Macrae, Stangor, & Hewstone, 1996). Messerschmidt argued that masculinity was therefore essential to explaining crime among men. Men assert their masculinity in a variety of ways including athleticism, sexual prowess, providing for one's family, educational and occupational attainment (Contreras, 2009; Evans, Gauthier, & Forsyth, 1998). Particularly relevant here however is the demonstration of masculinity through displays of toughness and a desire for respect (Anderson, 1999). Messerschmidt argued that while upper and middle-class males were able to use their comparatively higher incomes that their superior education and careers afforded them, to establish their masculinity, lower class males had fewer legitimate opportunities to do so and were therefore more likely to turn to illegitimate means (Messerschmidt, 1993). One of the more common themes among Messerschmidt's (2000) interviews with young, male, violent offenders was the desire to prove themselves as 'real men'. These were boys that suffered bullying in school and ridicule as a result of their poverty and were in search of the respect of their peers. Britton (2011) noted that a recognition of the role that social inequality plays in the route that men take towards crime is not to say that the poor are inherently predisposed to criminality. Rather, crime occurs within a social context in which men feel intense pressure to achieve masculine status but lack the resources to do so.

Gendered explanations for male offending have therefore typically portrayed the image of the cunning strategist who makes the rational decision to engage in crime based on his masculine ideals (Parker & Maggard, 2005). By contrast, women have been portrayed as being driven to crime as a result of issues relating to their psyche or through victimisation (Klein & Kreis, 1976). While feminist and pro-feminist interrogations into female crime have been critical to the advancement of knowledge on the subject, they too have tended to support the lack of agency among female offenders, through a focus on the role of victimisation. Ritchie (1996) advanced the theory of gender entrapment to explain how women are pushed towards criminal involvement as a result of a combination of expected gender roles, intimate partner violence and their social position. She argued that the realities of living in poverty were compounded by the violence faced in their daily lives at the hands of intimate partners ultimately resulting in a transition to criminal activity. Indeed, many scholars have linked women's involvement in crime to a host of difficult life circumstances including poverty, drug use and childhood or adult physical and/or sexual abuse (Chesney-Lind & Rodriguez, 1983; Chesney-Lind & Shelden, 1992; Maher, 1997). Work in the area of shoplifting is instructive as it relates to empirical depictions of male offending motivations. It has been commonly concluded that stealing is a manifestation of a desire to display one's masculinity and as such, men steal items that are of no particular use to them (Steffensmeier & Allan, 1996). Such crimes served to increase masculine capital within an environment that glorified toughness (Alder & Polk, 1996; Hochstetler & Copes, 2003; Katz, 2000; Messerschmidt, 1993; Mullins, 2006; Oliver, 1994; Winlow, 2001). Men, they argued, used crime, and in particular, street crime, in order to enhance their manhood among their peers on the streets. Shoplifting at the hands of women however has highlighted the role of necessity, based on financial hardships including child rearing responsibilities (Allen, 1987; Heidensohn, 1994).

Davies (1999) argued for the need for more nuance in theorising about gendered motivations to offend. She lamented an empirical culture in which for years, with little exception, greed and economic gain had been deemed sufficient to explain male involvement in crime. Indeed, the propensity to depict male offenders as being in complete control of their criminal decision making, while attributing little or no agency to that of women, has been one of the more enduring characteristics of research on crime (Covington, 1985; Pettiway, 1987; Steffensmeier, 1980). It is important to recognise the problematic nature of such binary representations. The assumption that victimisation and/or child rearing responsibilities are exclusive to women and that more strategic autonomous motives characterise the offending of men fails to recognise the complex and dynamic nature of offending. These representations, though not without relevance, are inadequate, since they fail to accept that, for example among men, there exist offenders for whom familial responsibilities may in fact be the main motivating factor. There have long been calls therefore to expand criminological discourse beyond these binary linkages in order to truly understand the complex factors involved in criminal offending (Allen, 1987; Maher, 1997). This manuscript argues that the reluctance to accept that male offending may at times extend beyond self-serving motivations, towards those related to familial responsibilities, is due to the patriarchal assumption that child rearing is the domain of women.

Poverty in the Caribbean

Criminal offending operates against the background of high levels of poverty across much of the Caribbean. Indeed, this has been the case throughout recent history. The deployment of the West Indian Royal Commission in August 1938 signalled the urgent concern for poverty in the region and the desire to improve the living standards of citizens of the British Caribbean. Conditions at the time had precipitated a series of labour unrests and the Commission was designed to investigate the concerns, as well as to make recommendations for alleviating them. The report of the Commission shed light on the sub-standard living conditions that were being experienced by large numbers of persons in the region (Potter, Barker, Conway, & Klak, 2014). The work of the commission was one of the first extensive research studies into poverty in the region.

Since 1995, the Caribbean Development Bank (CDB) has commissioned a series of Country Poverty Assessments (CPA)/Country Assessments of Living Conditions (CALC) throughout Caribbean member states. The main objective has been to establish the level, severity and characteristics of poverty in the Caribbean to facilitate the development of strategies and policies that would effectively reduce poverty. Notwithstanding recent improvements in rates of unemployment and living standards, today, rates of poverty within the region remain relatively high with at least one in five persons living below the poverty threshold (UNDP, 2016). This presents major challenges for regional development. Data suggest that within the Eastern Caribbean for example, the incidence of poverty (individual) is particularly high in countries such as St Kitts (23.7%), Nevis (15.9%), St Lucia (28.8%) and Grenada (37.5%) (Downes, 2010). Rates of poverty do vary considerably among countries throughout the region however. Haiti, for example, has the highest rate of poverty in the Caribbean with seven out of every ten persons estimated to be living in poverty. By contrast, it is estimated that only one out of every eight persons in Barbados is living in below the poverty line (Puryear & Malloy-Jewers, 2009).

Bourne (2005) identified four features of poverty that characterise the region: (1) greater levels of poverty exist in rural areas despite
urban poverty being more destabilising; (2) low levels of education
among poor households precipitate a lack of participation in labour
markets; (3) wage inequalities create a working poor that struggles to
survive on their wages leading to a form of exclusion just as damaging
as unemployment; and (4) there are high levels of poverty among the
elderly. In addition to overall levels of poverty, the relative deprivation experienced by some sections of Caribbean society is a cause for
concern. Recent government policies such as structural adjustment
programmes and free market models have been instrumental in increasing levels of inequality to a considerable degree (Leighton, 2012).
Large-scale unemployment, the growth of the informal economy and
low wages are only some of the negative effects. There have been several recent studies of the quality of life of minimum-wage workers.
Henry-Lee examined the coping strategies of one of the most rapidly
growing groups of workers in Jamaica, security guards. She found that
their wages did not allow them to meet the cost of basic necessities,
and they were forced to reduce expenditure on food and to eat fewer
meals, to walk instead of use public transportation and to rely on re-
mittances from relatives abroad. Some of their wives withdrew from
the labour market since the wages of the women could not cover the
cost of child care and transportation (Henry-Lee, 2002). Added to this
are concerns relating to the recent economic crisis. Countries such as
Jamaica that are heavily dependent on tourism are facing an extremely
difficult situation (Weisbrot, 2011). Despite recent decreases, inequality in Latin America and the Caribbean as a region remains the largest
in the world (Cornia, 2010).

Summary

As discussed earlier, the theory of bounded rationality suggests that
extra-legal considerations play a significant role in the decision-making
process of those involved in law enforcement. Simon (1976), referring
specifically to judges, argued that the sentencing process is both complicated and challenging. As a result, Judges develop strategies that
assist in the decision-making process. Hawkins (1981) too sought to
explain disparities in sentencing in a similar manner. He suggested
that time constraints meant that judges rely on what has been referred
to as a perceptual shorthand, based on assumptions and stereotypes
that they themselves apply to offenders. Such assumptions and stereotypes are linked to a variety of characteristics that may include race,

age, economic status and particularly relevant to this manuscript – that of gender. Steffensmeier (1980) argued that members of the judiciary attached a significant level of importance to the responsibilities associated with being the primary caretaker of dependent children. As such, this manuscript argues therefore that those who are deemed to be responsible for this primary care benefit from an assumption among the general citizenry and members of the justice system that criminal acts are committed against the background of this care. These assumptions are guided by patriarchal stereotypes which mean that women are the ones expected to be responsible for primary care, and so are deemed more integral to the development of children than men who are assumed to be often times absent.

3 Gender and family relations in Barbados and the Caribbean

Caribbean family life has been uniquely shaped by a logical heritage, the experience of slavery and colonialism, multi-racial and multicultural societies and by the socio-economic context of migration, unemployment and poverty. The myth of Caribbean women as black, strong, powerful matriarchs has been espoused for centuries (Barrow, 1986). Many of the studies on Caribbean women have looked at women within the broader research on family, and this has shaped women's positioning in state and institutional policies and practices, including how they are perceived by state institutions and the law. The discursive space of womanhood is a gendered enclosure of reinforcement and resistance where its instrumentalisation occurs within a set of complex power relations. This instrumentalisation reinforces gendered assumptions of the sexual division of labour where the woman's place is seen to be in the home with her primary role being that of mother; and the father's role being that of financial contributor, often exempted from domestic and child care activities. In this chapter I begin with a broad discussion of the critical contributions of Caribbean gender scholars. I then provide a detailed review of Caribbean gender and family relations, looking more specifically at the Barbadian context. This is important as it is the background against which those interviewed in this study (magistrates, police, citizens) that affect whether or not an offender is incarcerated were raised.

Critical contributions of Caribbean gender scholars

Early eighteenth- and nineteenth-century feminist thought occurred at a time when Caribbean women were still enslaved and seen as property of the plantation owner. In fact, there was no research or overt women's movements occurring in the Caribbean around that time. These early feminist theorisings are criticised for being exclusively based on the experiences of middle-class white women (Mohanty & Alexander, 1997). They are also criticised for being homogenous in their conclusions and lacking any originality in their application. Some argue that they merely inserted women issues into male dominant theories, which in itself proved problematic (Grewal & Kaplan, 1994).

Surfacing from the fight for all men to be included in the vote, gender became a prominent issue from the 1960s onwards. Women began speaking out against the inequality they experienced based on their sex, race and class. Their unity with men as they fought for the right to vote resulted in women recognising their own subordination and inequality as a human. Consequently, women began forming groups, educating themselves and each other, and fighting against the gender inequality and injustice. Thus, the term 'second wave feminism' was coined by Marsha Lear who used it to describe women's group in the United States, Britain and Europe that linked women's ideas to those that informed the right to vote. They attempted to move beyond striving for rights to be extended to women in the public sphere, to address the so-called personal/private issues of reproduction, sexuality and cultural representation that affected women in their everyday lives. Still these western writings which emerged out of second wave feminism falsely portray all Third World women as the same, ignoring the differences and the complexity of their experiences (Mohanty & Alexander, 1997).

While the battle for equality between men and women was occurring in a formal sense in the north, Caribbean women too were fighting for equality and justice. For Caribbean women, the early fights were not fought in academia but in the form of resistance. Antrobus (2004) identifies this resistance manifesting in several ways including outright refusal to work, damage of plantation property, infanticide and riots. This type of fight which was central to Caribbean women's race, class and history is a point of departure from international women's struggles which is crucial to an understanding of Caribbean women's issues and gender relations. Integral to this early struggle is the notion of strength which characterises Caribbean women and also which led to them being inaccurately labelled as 'matriarchal'. But this 'inner power' which early Caribbean women exemplified, while appearing to stem from a sense of security in one's self, a necessary factor in bettering women's situation, has resulted in the invisibility of women's struggles, and hence, a lack of government's assistance in promoting gender equality in this regard (Barriteau, 2003). These unequal power relations characterise the notion gender. Barriteau (2002, p. 30) defines gender as:

> . . .complex systems of personal and social relations of domination and power through which women and men socially create and maintain and through which they gain access to, or are allocated status, power and material resources within society.

There are ideological and material components of gender equality which shape and affect each other. These 'gendered norms' govern behaviours and attitudes that, in turn, produce and regulate state laws and practices (Mohammed, 1995).

Black nationalist global movements such as the human rights movement and the black power movement saw Caribbean women in the forefront fighting for a new sense of freedom. Sprouting from this battle was the realisation of the gender inequality which existed, and the problems which primarily affected women. The year 1985 was a very critical point for feminism. It was in this year that the third United Nations (UN) World Conference on Women was held in Nairobi, Kenya. It consisted of both an intergovernmental conference and a forum of non-governmental organisations which brought together women from across the globe who shared their experiences with and criticisms of new economic policies, conservative governments and cultural political movements that they deemed inimical to women's interests (Moghadam, 2005).

The early feminist movements were influenced by liberalism and therefore succumbed to similar shortcomings. Early women's movements argued for equality for women on the grounds of morality as well as the notion that it would benefit the family and society as a whole (Antrobus, 2006), focusing on specific issues in the society. Nonetheless, it was fuelled by the global women's movement which provided it with some impetus for change. It is important to understand the formation and processes involved in the women's movement because they provided the foundation for the development of a feminist movement in the Caribbean.

Many early women's movements had political agendas and reiterated the gender roles which feminists fought against. According to Antrobus (2004) women's movements differed from other movements in that they were crosscutting, asked different questions and often sought goals that challenged conventional definitions of where women wanted to go. However, even in their fight for gender equality, they perpetuated the injustices of gender relations as they failed to challenge the ideology and instead focused on gender identity politics and were concerned primarily with social transformation (Barriteau, 2003).

These movements supported the implementation of equal opportunity for women to access education, which, in turn, provided knowledge of feminist theories which informed Caribbean research and policies. These movements were different from other social movements and can be defined by diversity, their global reach, and method of organising, but lacked homogeneity, common objectives, continuity, unity and coordination (Antrobus, 2004). Early feminism in the Caribbean merely sought to apply traditional theories to Caribbean women's experiences. This work aided in the implementation of many projects and policies, one of which is the Women in Development (WID), which was an attempt to integrate women into development. The approach was preoccupied with women's position as producers. It ignored the impact of global inequalities on women in developing countries and rarely addressed questions of women's insubordination, race and class. Although women were now involved in development, it was nevertheless in an exploitative position. Resultantly, Women and Development (WAD) emerged in the 1970s as a means of correcting this critique of WID (Beneria & Sen, 1981). They had a more radical approach as they sought to separate women's issues and projects from men's. However, they too fell prey to the critique of homogenising women. Hence, in the 1980s, Gender and Development (GAD) became the prime issue as they explored how women in developing countries are affected on a local, regional and global level; and looked at the relationship between men and women.

As more research in the Caribbean emerged, organisations began to adapt. This was aided by the fact that unlike women's movements, these feminist projects had a common objective and were united. Moreover, the global women's movement created an international platform from which women's issues could be launched as global restructuring was affecting women internationally. In the United States, global restructuring manifested in the form of Reaganism; in the United Kingdom it was in the form of Thatcherism; and in the Caribbean and other developing countries it was in the form of structural adjustment. Consequently, women began to feel the negative effects of the global economic policies. Suddenly, women were now responsible for everything the state previously provided, and without any improvement in their financial position. Hence, in the late 1980s Guy Standing[1] coined the term 'Feminization of Labour' to explain this position. Standing argued that

> . . . the increasing globalisation of production and the increasing pursuit of flexible forms of labour to retain or increase competitiveness, as well as changing job structures in industrial enterprises,

favoured the 'feminisation of employment" in the dual sense of an increase in the numbers of women in the labour force and a deterioration of work conditions (labour standards, income, and employment status).

(Moghadam, 2005, p. 5)

This is reflective of what was happening in the Caribbean in the 1980s; but prior to that, Caribbean women faced similar conditions and struggled to have them addressed. Thus, Caribbean women's history cannot be excluded from an analysis of globalisation's impact on them, as the new challenges faced were merely a decorated/revamped version of what they fought against years prior. This exploitation is very much the same as it was prior to independence. Thus, like the earlier forms of resistance and movements, women became aware of their separateness as women, their alienation, marginalisation, isolation and even abandonment within a broader movement for social justice and change, all occurring on a global scale (Antrobus, 2004). This 'conscientization'[2] and struggle for agency fuelled the global women's movement.

Research is a major component of policy formation. Emerging from international feminism and the decade of women (1975–1985) conferences was scholarship focused on Caribbean women and the notion of 'Caribbean feminism'. Traditional feminist theories were decomposed to assess their suitability in explaining Caribbean women's experience. These studies were guided by whatever theory of development was most dominant at the time. Therefore, liberal theory became the basis of policy which sought to better women's circumstances. The theory valued market forces as the primary determinant of development and posited the idea of equality for all (Giroux, 2008). The transplanting of this theory (which surfaced from the enlightenment period) to explain Caribbean women's experience was inadequate. It is, however, a fundamental starting point for feminists as they advocate for gender equality and justice in the Caribbean.

Caribbean gender and family relations

Caribbean gender scholars have examined the experiences of women primarily through an exploration of their position within the family and development. They began with a critique of early Western anthropological studies, accounting for the colonial, cultural, economic, political and gendered relations. Anthropological studies of the family in the Caribbean from the 1940s through the 1960s generally described the Caribbean family as dysfunctional, compared to European and

North American nuclear family models. However, later research of the 1970s and 1980s recognised that Caribbean family patterns had been largely consistent since the days of slavery, and that they were in fact functional in terms of child and family survival under the conditions of colonial and post-colonial poverty and oppression. The early nineteenth and late twentieth century depicted a different kind of family life for Caribbean women.

Early theories showed little comprehension of the diversity of Caribbean families and failed to account for the colonial influence on the family structures. Heterogeneous families are influenced by culture and religious beliefs with most being of African descent and character-ised by a high rate of non-nuclear arrangements with the mother-child bond prioritised over heterosexual bonds (Mohammed & Perkins, 1999; Senior, 1991).

Parsons and Bales (1956), sceptical of the argument that Caribbean family is dysfunctional, argued instead that the family had undergone a process of 'specialization and differentiation'. They noted that the most important function performed by the family is the stabilisation of the adult personality and the socialisation of children. This takes place through a four-fold model that constitutes the structure of the family (nuclear). They argued that there were certain universal social prereq-uisites of 'normal' personality development, particularly those related to the existence of sexuality in infants and the sexual attributes of par-ents. Since, for them, these were universal and inescapable, the groups in which personality formation takes place, which was usually the fam-ily, would have to be organised on primarily descriptive lines – that is, in terms of 'natural' attributes that an individual cannot control. Here emerged the belief in the naturalness and fixed familial roles of women and men which continue to be internalised and reproduced, despite the theory being refuted by the experiences of Caribbean families.

Western notions of the ideal family, as exemplified by Parsons and Bales, eventually proved problematic in the Caribbean as our history exposed different types of familial patterns. But more importantly, women were so much at the forefront of the family that some aca-demics labelled the Caribbean's primary family as 'matriarchal'. The term matriarch suggests that women exercise a degree of power and control not only in their familial network but also within a wider so-cial context (Rowley, 2002). This stereotypical term has been deemed unworthy and untrue of Caribbean households as it denotes the do-minion of the mother over family and state (Rosaldo & Lamphere, 1974). Therefore this suggests that an overarching system of female dominance exists in the Caribbean when in fact the Caribbean family is predominantly female headed (but not exclusive of men), and this influence does not translate into the public sphere. Although sometimes used interchangeably, this is in contrast to 'matrifocality' which refers to the female centredness of families, such that matrifocality can exist even when men are present in the household (Rowley, 2002). This distinction postulates that in essence matriarchy was non-existent in the Caribbean. Rowley explores the concepts of matriarchy and matrifocality in the reality of Caribbean women through the method of narrative discourse. She speaks of an Afro-maternal subject of Caribbean feminism, where mothering is central to Caribbean women's concept of self; and where this subject is shaped through the management of women's lives, and the range of meanings and discourses that circulate around women's bodies, particularly those of mothering (Rowley, 2003). Historical accounts of women in the Caribbean illustrate how their gendering was seen in the sexualisation of their black bodies and the exploitation of reproduction, more so than their physical and manual labour. Hence, motherhood became a symbol or marker of womanhood, and became central to the family unit.

One of the first anthropological studies in the Caribbean was done by R.T. Smith who described Caribbean societies as matrifocal in nature. In doing so, Smith was making reference not to female dominance or headship, but to the mother-centredness of Caribbean families (Smith, 1996). Smith maintained the image of femininity prescribed by the model in which women are to assume demeanours of modesty and obedience. He asserted that women exhibit proper standards of sexual fidelity and morality and desire marriage as an indicator of enhanced social status. Clarke contested this assertion in presenting Caribbean families as primarily single headed female households, in which the women were more focused on their children than intimate partner (Clarke, 1966). Although women spent a greater part of their time within their own house and daily routine, they nevertheless engaged in various income earning activities which revolved around the domestic sphere.

Smith's homogenous theorising assumes that Caribbean families comprise both man and woman, suggesting that women remain in the home and men go out to work thereby affording them the position to make important decisions within the family. Caribbean scholars demonstrate through their studies that women were the primary decision makers in the household even when men were present (Anderson, 1986; Barrow, 2001; Clarke, 1966; Lazarus-Black, 2001).

The discourse of parental roles which posits that the mother is the primary care provider of the children, home and family, while the father is the breadwinner, has persisted through early to contemporary scholarship (Barrow, 1986; Evans & Davies, 1997; Senior, 1991), and has shaped state and institutional policies (Robinson, 2003). Children are required to be obedient, respectful and submissive to their parents. Girls are expected to assist with domestic chores around the house, whereas boys are expected to do activities outside the house, such as taking care of the yard and running errands (Barrow, 1986). However, historically, Caribbean women have simultaneously taken care of the home and provided financially for their family with or without the presence of men. There is indeed a clear pattern of resistance in the organisation of the family and household duties. The extent of this resistance across the Caribbean suggests that even as Caribbean men are involved in the affective and financial aspects of the family, their emotional availability and social ties to children are unclear (Sharpe, 1996). While the resistance comes from both men and women, they still exist within the accepted cultural norm of a society which privileges men even when they fall short of their expectations, but continuously subordinates women, often blaming them for whatever goes wrong in the family. This can be attributed to the patriarchal system as seen in the ideology which favours the role of men over women, and which places the burden of family primarily on the woman.

Most Eastern Caribbean islands boast family life based on African practices and beliefs, influenced by the colonial experience. There is however a mix of African and European culture in addition to adaptations required for survival that produces diverse family types and practices. Early Sociological studies position the family as the core of any society; it is where norms and values are transferred from generation to generation; and where the system of exploitation was sustained through the continuous reproduction practices. The perpetuation of the sexual division of labour was also visible during slavery. The colonial experience demonstrates that even when enslaved women were seen as chattel/property/unhuman, engaging in similar activities as enslaved men, child care remained solely the job of enslaved black women (Shepherd, 1999). Enslaved black women were often labelled 'bad mothers' as the planter class was not familiar with their West African practices which were thwarted by their experience of slavery (Barrow, 1986; Bush, 1990). While black women continued to engage in traditional African practices after emancipation, there was also a shift towards engaging in activities that were practiced by the whites and labelled 'good'. Such activities were racially, economically and class specific and thus proved challenging for black women who had to work in and outside the home.

Brereton (1998) describes a situation in which an enslaved woman got married to a free black man, making her masters furious. According to Brereton's research, "they could not tolerate her assertion of a right to a separate and autonomous personal and sexual life" (Brereton, 1998, p. 156). Thus, the enslaved married woman was flogged and eventually forced to move with her masters to England, leaving her husband in the Caribbean. Enslaved women had no private life as they were owned by their masters; their personal family was not recognised by their owners. More importantly, these women lacked a sense of autonomy and empowerment. Their lives were public as their private choices were disrespected and often ignored. Women had no control or hold on their children or their male partners, and many fought for their rights through infanticide, riots and suicide.

Caribbean women's experiences of slavery defied European norms on ideal femininity. During slavery women had to work in the fields or plantation house, plant their own food and take care of their family (Beckles, 1998). Safa (1995) notes that what current researchers label 'inside' and 'outside' work has been an aspect of Caribbean women's lives since colonialism. Moreover, women sold the surplus food from their home gardens to earn money and this was the origin of the market system which is such a vital part of the region's economy to date (Beckles & Shepherd, 2000).

Given the living conditions of the time (late eighteenth to early nineteenth century), as well as the family structure (some men were absent and sometimes the father was unknown), mothers were primarily responsible for the care of their children. However, a woman was still expected to perform her job on the plantation in order to fulfil her obligations to the plantation owner. Additionally, in order to provide food and clothes for her family (since the plantation owner merely provided one suit of clothes) she planted her own garden and made clothes for her children (Beckles & Shepherd, 2000). All these private tasks were expected to be completed after she performed her plantation duty. She was also expected to teach her children certain skills and chores.

After emancipation, while the fathers continued to work outside the home, the mothers raised the children, took care of the home and engaged in farming and other domestic chores as a means of earning extra income (Mair, 2006). The sexual division of labour was perpetuated through socialisation as mothers often taught their daughters house care, and their sons were tasked with 'outdoors' activities such as farming (Clarke, 1966). Yet, girls were also taught to engage in farming in the form of caring for a kitchen garden and animals such as chickens, cows, sheep, thus associating the same task with domestic chores. Tied to these ideas of womanhood was the marker of mother-hood and more specifically the concept of 'good mother', as Caribbean mothers who sacrificed for the welfare of their children were seen as 'good mothers'. The value ascribed to this 'sacrifice' affects how the actions of mothers are perceived by the society.

The problem that arises with early theorising on the Caribbean fam-ily is that these stereotypes and standardised portrayals of women are distorted and misconceived (Barrow & Reddock, 2001). They present a pattern of submissiveness, a preoccupation with home, motherhood and domesticity and the economic security derived from dependence on a man which is highly unlikely in the circumstances of poverty, unemployment and economic uncertainty in which many Caribbean women live. The criticisms made illustrate how women hold a key po-sition in the family structure even with the presence of a man.

The early Caribbean Creole family form was primarily based on a visiting relationship, whereby the man was a part of another household but had his family at another location (Clarke, 1966). This evolved into a cohabiting relationship whereby the man and woman lived together but was not married. As these relationships broke down, it often re-sulted in the man leaving the home, and the children remaining with the mother, who often became the head of the household, resulting in the Caribbean's female-headed culture. According to Clarke (Clarke, 1966, p. iv), "among the Creoles, nuclear or elementary families are systematically fragmented and dispersed throughout two or more households as a direct effect of their mating organization". Therefore, family and household became complicated and blurred.

Clarke's work reflects the typical Jamaican family as single parent and matrifocal and proposes that Caribbean women's role in post-colonial societies involves both nurturing and instrumental tasks. One can argue that this can be generalised to most of the English-speaking West Indian territories as Caribbean women have been managing multiple activities for decades. Additionally, the jobs culture, salaries and production expectations in the Caribbean vary significantly from other parts of the world. It means that mothering is done differently and at times singularly in the Caribbean and therefore North Ameri-can and Western theories cannot adequately explore Caribbean wom-en's experiences.

The strong post-colonial kinship network allowed Caribbean women to engage in both income earning and social reproduction ac-tivities. These networks, which made black women key figures, were a part of the development of survival strategies (Carby, 1997). Given their low wage jobs, Afro-Caribbean women could not have taken care of their family and paid for child care; thus, they relied on extended family and the community to assist (Barrow, 1986). In fact, mothers often left the public sphere when there was a breakdown in child care arrangements.

Senior (1991) described Caribbean mothering as a set of activities, cultural beliefs and practices. Using the data collected from the Women in the Caribbean Project (WICP), she examined women's lives and work in 14 Caribbean countries and demonstrated the manner in which motherhood was perceived as natural, and as an indicator of womanhood. She focused on how cultural norms shape perceptions and practices of family, motherhood and work. The WICP was one of the first extensive multi-disciplinary studies done in the Eastern Caribbean to examine the lives of women. This study highlighted the gender inequality perpetuated in Caribbean society, through the experiences of Caribbean women over the period 1979–1982 (Anderson, 1986). The data from this project comprised five issues: social reproduction and women's dual roles, women as domestic brokers, female leadership and decision making, sex-role identity and self-perception, and relationships with males. The project examined "women's productive and reproductive roles in society and the emphasis of women's contribution to economic development" (Anderson, 1986, p. 298), noting specifically how women conceptualised work as anything necessary to ensure the upkeep of both themselves and their households, thereby suggesting the multiple and non-linear responsibilities of women.

The approach of Caribbean feminists has been to examine the experiences of Caribbean women as distinct from that of black women in different geographical locations (especially in North America). For scholars such as Barrow and Reddock (2001), Caribbean feminism is unique in that it emerges from a history of colonialism and resistance, along with an intersectionality of issues such as race, class, ethnicity, religion and gender. It challenges the "systemic nature of patriarchy rather than individual males" (Mohammed, 2003, p. 19), thus disrupting essentialist notions that plagued first and second wave feminism. Rhoda Reddock and Smith (2008) highlighted how mothering was taken for granted when referring to women and work. They argued that from slavery, black women have struggled to be recognised first as human and then as equal to men. Their struggles have compromised their roles as women, wives, girlfriends and mothers; it has brought into question the ideal versus the gendered expectations. Mair (2006) too depicted a similar feature in her work on Jamaican women.

While Barriteau (2004) shares a similar perspective, writing from a political science background, she advocates for a postmodern feminist approach. She argues that a Caribbean feminist approach must recognise difference, organise political action based on both differences and commonalities and acknowledge the gendered nature of social relations. These early scholars explore the intersectionality of various issues when researching the experience of Caribbean women and create the foundation for a Caribbean feminist theorising. Mohammed and Perkins (1999), for example, highlighted the variations in women's experiences based on class and ethnicity. They demonstrated how class impacted the experiences of women especially as it related to their level of education. Women who had at least secondary level education often sought to further their studies in some way (once possible), and as a result were more knowledgeable about certain issues. This education afforded them a sense of pride and empowerment which propelled them into becoming agents in their societies. Mohammed and Perkins' study recorded how working-class women saw education as a means out of poverty for their children, and thus they did everything possible to ensure their children received a good education. Their findings, like the others, demonstrated women's subordinate position in society and the gendered norms that shape the experiences, perceptions and practices.

Mohammed (2003) credits second wave feminism for the benefits which third wave feminists enjoy today. She spoke to the impact on perceptions noting that as a result of second wave feminism, "feminism is no longer a concentrated set of ideas shared by a specific group or individual who advocate for rights for women", but an internalised gender consciousness (Mohammed, 2003, p. 2). Mohammed further notes that the shift in the global political economy and technology in the twentieth century has resulted in a change in the climate and methods of resistance and struggle in organised social movements.

Men and women exist within a gender system based on constructed ideologies of masculinity and femininity. These ideologies affect access to material resources, creating unequal relations between men and women, and resulting in the oppression of women (Barritteau, 2004). Hence, women's navigation of their roles and responsibilities within such a system is inherently burdened.

The Barbados experience

Barbados (the setting of the research) consists of a predominantly black population. Although it too experienced the scars of slavery, the organisation of the household in comparison to that of its neighbours is contrasting. While there are similar household composition and family types in the Anglophone Caribbean, the degree to each type differs among the islands. Thus, in Barbados the extended family is quite prevalent (Barbados Country Assessment of Living Conditions, 2010).

The shared colonial experience within the Anglophone Caribbean produces shared gender ideologies, structures and practices. The distinctiveness of Barbadian women's experience lies in their reaction to the inequality which can be garnered from Chamberlain's examination of gender as a factor in nation building (Chamberlain, 2010). As one of the poorest British territories in the Caribbean, during the 1930s Barbados experienced the lowest life expectancy in the region, highest child mortality and considerable unemployment. Between 1937 and 1966, women comprised the majority of Barbadian population and the majority of workers. Like the rest of the Caribbean, women were the primary breadwinners as well as the household heads, raising generations in 'conservative religious beliefs' but with "empowering faith practices. . . which reinforced a togetherness, a kind of covert manifestation of identity (Chamberlain, 2010, p. 18)". This religious foundation provided the basis of the family and community operations and management.

The 1995–2010 period in Barbados saw improvements in living conditions with steady but moderate economic growth and a falling rate of unemployment. The global economic recession of 2001(after 911 in the United States) and 2008/2009 (worldwide recession which again began in the United States) affected the island significantly causing a decline in output and a rise in unemployment creating transient poverty (Barbados Country Assessment of Living Conditions, 2010). The main growth areas were in the non-tradable sectors, namely construction, distribution and transportation. The 2010 Country Assessment of Living Conditions (CALC) indicated that the poverty line in Barbados was BDS$5,503 per capita per year, and approximately 7,000 households in Barbados existed on income below this threshold. Nonetheless, in the region, Barbados has the lowest percentage of persons affected by poverty – only 13.9 per cent of the population. Female-headed households however represent nearly 60 per cent of poor households nationally.

As women make progress in attaining certain degrees of equality, there is a trend whereby women's career opportunities are improving relative to where they were, but this does not translate into gender equity (Blossfeld & Hofmeister, 2006). While there is an increase in the number of women in the labour market, there is also a reduction in the quality of their employment. Although we are seeing more and more women in the Caribbean surpassing men in numbers at the University of the West Indies, one cannot say that this has translated to the world of work. In fact, there are still few women in the upper echelons of organisations in Barbados (CARICOM, 2003). Women in the Caribbean, especially Barbados, began to explore the field of education which became available to them (and in the case of Barbados, free). Thus the 1990s (especially late 1990s) saw an impetus of women into the University of the West Indies, and other training program. They believed that this was a meaningful way out of poverty and means by which they can compete with men for the limited jobs available. According to the 2010 National Census in Barbados, 1,307 females between the age of 20 and 24 were studying full-time while 875 were studying part time; As the age increased so did the number of part time female students so that the 25–29 category saw 371 full-time, 936 part time; and the over 30 years' age group saw 582 full-time and 3,178 part-time female students. While definitive conclusions cannot be drawn from just the figures, it suggests that more women are engaging in part time work to accommodate their personal, professional and academic career. On the contrary, this is not reflected in the salaries as the Barbados census report shows that despite women's educational attainment, more men are in the higher salary brackets than women (Barbados Statistical Services, 2013). It suggests that gender inequality is very much present and despite materialistic strides, the limited ideological change prevents the attainment of gender equity.

Summary

Family structures and practices have been impacted by the household composition, the financial circumstances and modernism (enlightenment through education; politics). However, the underlying ideology persists through the expectations of the society. It is still expected that the father will be the principal economic provider for the home and the mother will be responsible for the social care of the family. Caribbean scholarship on women and families illustrates the complexities of women's engagement in income earning, domestic and child care activities. Amidst global advocacy for the presence of both parent within families, and changes to the sexual division of labour, women are still positioned as the primary care taker of the domestic sphere and children.

This gender ideology is engrained through socialisation and informs policies, legislature and cultural practices. Discourses around womanhood and manhood produce and regulate the behaviour of men and women, affect their access to material resources and impact their social, economic, political and gendered relations.

Notes

1 Guy Standing is an International Labour Organisation economist.
2 Bell Hooks and Peggy Antrobus define 'conscientization' as a process of reflection and action that has helped to mobilise women to challenge neo-liberal and fundamentalist state policies at national and global levels. Lorde posits that it means breaking our silence – those conditioned by privilege and those rooted in fear. For Audre Lorde, it is silence above all that immobilises us (Lorde, 1984, p. 44).

4 The intersection between male offending, civil society and the police

In this chapter I examine relations between male offenders and civil society in the form of shop owners/managers, as well as interactions between male offenders and the police. A total of 20 shop owners/proprietors were selected for in-depth interview from a sample of retail stores of various types and sizes in the Central Business District (CBD) of the city of Bridgetown, Barbados, including the two largest retail stores on Broad Street. This is the main shopping area in Barbados. In addition, focus group sessions were held with male and female members of the Royal Barbados Police Force (RBPF).

Shoplifting

Shoplifting is commonly defined as "theft from the selling floor while a store is open for business" (Francis, 1979, p. 10). Often referred to in several jurisdictions as 'wilful concealment', shoplifting in Barbados is recorded by the RBPF as 'theft from shops/stores' under the general classification of 'Theft and Theft Related Crimes'. Table 4.1 shows the total cases of shoplifting reported to the police from 2016 to 2019.[1]

The study of shoplifting has generally proven to be problematic, primarily as a result of the low percentage of offenders who are apprehended and turned over to law enforcement, despite the serious problem it poses to the business community. Indeed, Hollinger and Davis (2002) found that among their sample of retailers, only 24 per cent

Table 4.1 Theft from shops/stores (shoplifting) 2016–2018

	2016	2017	2018
Theft from shops/stores	168	128	169

Source: Royal Barbados Police Force.

of all shoplifters that were caught were prosecuted. Similarly, it has been suggested that as many as two-thirds of all thefts go unreported (NCVS, 2012). As a result, it is argued by some that no other crime is as severely under-reported as shoplifting (Dabney, Hollinger, & Dugan, 2004; Hollinger & Davis, 2002).

Because of the unreliability of official data, therefore, scholars have turned to victimisation or self-report studies in an attempt to obtain a more accurate representation of the prevalence of shoplifting. A number of these have found shoplifting to be among the most prevalent of all forms of criminality with many people admitting to have stolen something from a store at some point in their lives (Loeber, Farrington, Stouthamer-Loeber, & Van Kammen, 1998; Puzzanchera, 2000). The extent of the problem in Europe was highlighted by Bamfield (2004) who reported that over 1.2 million offenders were apprehended for shoplifting across a 16-country sample while Uniform Crime Reports estimated 1.2 million incidents of shoplifting in the United States in 2014 (Federal Bureau of Investigation, 2014). Prevalence has also been measured by assessing the level of financial loss incurred both on a macro and micro level (see Farmer & Dawson, 2017 for a review). Hollinger and Davis (2002) concluded that the average retail business owner suffers losses amounting to 1.7 per cent of gross sales revenue due to shoplifting and other forms of theft. Research in India and Pakistan has revealed national losses of as much as US$1.6 billion with the theft of items such as smart phones and computers increasing dramatically (Sharma, 2010). Similarly, unofficial figures in Russia point to losses of approximately US$26 million (Davidson, 2015). Perhaps the largest financial losses, however, have been incurred by the United States with an estimated annual loss of approximately US$10–13 billion (Farmer & Dawson, 2017).

Research on the nature and prevalence of shoplifting in the Caribbean is virtually absent from the criminological literature. However, one study found theft to be the most common form of victimisation among their sample of Jamaican businesses, considerably affecting day-to-day operations (Francis, Gibbison, Harriott, & Kirton, 2009). Theft of goods accounted for 43 per cent of all thefts with 27 per cent of businesses reporting that they were victimised on at least a quarterly basis.

Why are they stealing?

Despite the above-mentioned impacts, shoplifting, beyond attempts at assessing prevalence, has received relatively little attention by criminologists. The work of Cameron (1964) was pioneering in the field, as it represented the first major study on shoplifting motivations, and was used as a reference point for future scholarship. Using data from a Major Chicago department store, Cameron identified two categories of shoplifters. Boosters, forming 10 per cent of Cameron's sample of shoplifters, were part of an extended criminal subculture. These were professional shoplifters/thieves, stealing primarily for financial gain through re-sale. The remaining 90 per cent of Cameron's sample was termed as snitches. Although snitches were similar to Boosters in that they were chronic shoplifters, they were not part of any larger criminal network, and were otherwise law-abiding members of society. Although snitches were not desperately poor, stealing out of need, they were not stealing in order to re-sell.

Moore (1983) expanded upon the ideas of Cameron, and instead identified five types of shoplifters based on their varying motivations. The impulse shoplifter was very limited in his/her offending, stealing in an impromptu manner as opportunity arose, often targeting one relatively inexpensive item. Apprehension was followed by intense feelings of guilt. The occasional shoplifter was motivated primarily by group pressures, and stole between three and ten items during the course of a year. He/she did not take the offending seriously and if apprehended reacted with indifference. The episodic shoplifter was motivated by a desire for self-punishment. He/she offended in a sporadic manner often precipitated by bouts of depression or guilt. They targeted specific items and were generally compliant if apprehended. The fourth and most common type was the amateur shoplifter. For this category, shoplifting was an almost weekly activity motivated by its profitability. Offenders stole small items and were weighed against the risk of being caught. If apprehended they endeavoured to avoid prosecution by way of a variety of manipulation tactics. Finally, the semi-professional shoplifters used skilled techniques in order to offend with great frequency and were unique in their re-sale of stolen items. Although financial gain was the primary motivation, shoplifting served the added purpose of providing a reprieve from the societal injustices they believed they were experiencing on a daily basis.

An added dimension to research on shoplifting motivations emerges with the addition of gender as a variable of interest. There has been a prevailing belief that women display a higher propensity for involvement in shoplifting than men (see Dabney, Hollinger & Dugan, 2004 for a review), so much so that it has at times been referred to as a 'pink collar' crime (Caputo & King, 2011). A number of studies have however challenged this view (Flanagan & Maguire, 1990; HIndelang, 1974; Moschis, 1987) and contemporary scholarship has pointed to male overrepresentation in this form of offending, despite an increase in the representation of women in official statistics. Blanco et al. (2008) reported that among their US sample of 4,422 adult shoplifting offenders, 60 per cent were male. Indeed, the work of other scholars has revealed similar results (Dabney, Hollinger, & Dugan, 2004; Hirtenlehner, Blackwell, Leitgoeb, & Bacher, 2014). Within the literature on youth shoplifting too, although some studies have found higher levels of participation among girls (Wikstrom, Treiber, & Hardie, 2012), the majority have concluded that prevalence rates among boys are higher (Bamfield, 2012).

In Chapter 2 I referred to the manner in which research on the gendered motivations for shoplifting has tended to adhere to binary representations of male and female offending, whereby men steal as a mechanism of masculine capital accumulation or economic greed, while women steal out of necessity. Although both representations can be interpreted as evidence of rational offending (Krasnovsky & Lane, 1998), analysing women's involvement solely against the background of financial hardship presents them as victims, and thus removes any meaningful agency from their criminal participation and, critically for the purposes of this study, engenders greater feelings of sympathy towards them. In reality, both men and women are motivated to shoplift, by a variety of factors of which street capital, greed, economic gain and financial hardship may or may not form a part. An understanding of this is essential to the analysis that follows in this book, as the treatment of male offenders by citizens and law enforcement is often guided by the gendered assumptions made about male and female offending. Since the existence of economic explanations (agency) for male offending is generally accepted within the shoplifting literature, I will focus here instead on those explanations for women's involvement that run counter to the traditional lack thereof.

Caputo and King (2011) explored the conceptualisation of crime for the purposes of economic gain, as a form of work with characteristics similar to those of legitimate professions. Many of the skills necessary for success in the legitimate sphere – ability to learn, ability to adapt, ability to compete – are also honed through involvement in criminal pursuits (Letkemann, 1973). This type of theorising however has generally been applied to male offending. Miller (1978) represented one of the first attempts to see women involved in crime as 'working' for economic reward. He argued that women who engage in criminality for economic gain approach their involvement in a similar fashion to conventional workers. Contrary to the victimisation that characterises traditional depictions, these women make reasoned choices to offend, just as women in other professions too are guided by reason.

Indeed, the women in Caputo and King's (2011) study spoke of their shoplifting in occupational terms and approached it in ways tradition- ally thought to be masculine. Shoplifting was the mechanism chosen by these women as their 'criminal work specialisation' and in the ma- jority of cases was their primary source of income. The women were able to build up a customer base to whom they would sell their stolen goods for profit. In this way, they were able to meet their financial needs. In this sense, Caputo and King argued, women's involvement in shoplifting highlighted their individual agency, and in doing so, effectively transcended gender. When women challenge the gendered assumptions held as they relate to gender roles and activities, it neces- sitates a societal rethink of these roles. Miller (2002, p. 441) referred to this as 'challenging the gender dualism'. This subset of women shop- lifters therefore demonstrates the complexity of female criminal of- fending and is evidence of both their agency and their non-conformity (Caputo & King, 2011).

Gender role perceptions held by civil society and the police

In Chapter 2 I discussed the culturally assigned roles to which men and women typically gravitate. Embedded within these roles is the ex- pectation that everyone will conform. These patriarchal assumptions or expectations heavily influence interactions between male offenders, civil society and the police. At the heart of these assumptions is what societies view as masculine or feminine. Gilmore (1990) suggested three typical features of masculinity found in most societies: man the impregnator, man the provider and man the protector. Though not the only criterion for masculinity, it is clear that the notion of the male provider or breadwinner is central to constructions of masculinity in the Caribbean. Lewis (2004b) argued, however, that economic forces with the Caribbean had placed men at odds with traditional gender roles. Chronic unemployment and the relative strides made by women in the workforce meant that for large numbers of men fulfilling the role of breadwinner was an impossible task. Despite this struggle however, and despite the achievements of Caribbean women in the employment and educational spheres, the expectation remains that the primary role of men is to provide, while women are characterised by their ability to nurture and care for their families (Barrow, 1986; Dann, 1987). So much so has the Caribbean man accepted these la- bels that the notion of assuming the role of nurturer or caregiver is in direct opposition to his status as a man (Chevannes, 2001). As one of the participants in Chevannes' study among Jamaican men explained (Chevannes, 2001, p. 137):

> Most men think that 'gentle' is not macho, and that loving your children is strictly for females.

These patriarchal values are assimilated not only by Caribbean men, but indeed by wider society. Bailey and Coore-Desai (2012) found that Caribbean boys and girls saw the family unit in these terms. The most common role ascribed to men was that of provider. A man's primary role was to act as a breadwinner for the family, and he must be able to guarantee its financial security. One participant opined (p. 23):

> It's just like this, he must be the one who takes care of his family. He must be the one who brings money home.

The prevailing view was that a man should go out to work and support the family financially while his wife should stay at home and care for the children. Many participants believed that it was a woman's responsibility to act as a caregiver to the children, cook and clean the home, even if she had a job outside of the home. Similarly, Bailey, Branche, McGarritty and Stuart (1998) found that among young children in Jamaica, Dominica and Barbados, the expectation was that for women, their critical contribution to the family unit would manifest through their role as caregiver, while fathers were expected to assume the role of breadwinner. These findings are in keeping with what Momsen (1993) identified as the paradox of growing economic autonomy among women operating alongside entrenched patriarchy in that many mothers contributed to the financial upkeep of the home by way of employment; however they were nevertheless judged by their domestic functions.

This is the cultural context within which the business owners/proprietors and police officers involved in this study were raised. They were asked a number of questions with the aim of revealing the nature of their perceptions held about gender roles. Answers generally confirmed the subscription and adherence to very traditional views relating to the respective roles of men and women. The dominant view among the business owners interviewed was that the most important relationship within the family unit was that between a mother and her household. Brian, a 43-year-old store owner explained:

> Both my parents lived together when I was young. So I was able to see how they split duties in the household. I kind of carried

that with me as I got older and applied it to my own marriage. To me, the first thing is that they [women] must meet the needs of their husband, such as maintaining the physical state of the home, preparation of meals, reception of the husband. Things like that.

Robert, a 51-year-old store owner expressed similar sentiments:

Women, if married, should be supportive of the husband, and to be honest, that's what I looked for in a woman when I was ready to settle down.

Primary however among all her household functions was the role of a mother in the nurturing of her children. Women were responsible for both their physical and emotional well-being, allowing men to focus on financial support for the home. The contribution of women was seen as particularly critical in societies like Barbados, in which such a large percentage of households are headed by women. Indeed, much of the problems facing youth, and in particular young boys, were attributed by participants, to the failure of women, to fulfil their roles effectively. Barry, a 39-year-old store owner opined:

Without the attention of a mother you see a lot of crime, a lot of anger, a of disenchantment. They are very important for that. Love is what is missing from child development today and I is easier to tap into that in a woman than in a man.

The views too of Tracy, a 29-year-old store manager, were instructive:

As a woman I know there are things I am better suited for than a man. It's very obvious with children. If I am not around I would worry about my children. Many of the internal matters that cannot be fixed in children today are because of the absence of the mother. . . Human values and discipline are instilled into children from a young age by the mother. . . this is where the foundation is laid.

These views were indicative of a belief among participants that there existed an inherent predisposition among women for household duties. As far as children were concerned, this meant that the role of the woman in the home was more important than that of the man.

The views of the police officers interviewed were in direct accordance with those of the shop owners/proprietors. The officers spoke freely about the special bond that existed between them and their mothers, most of whom were still alive. They were generally raised in single parent, female-headed households and so saw themselves as well placed to assess the critical role played by mothers in the lives of their children. The experience of Brian was indicative:

> I grew up with my mother being my mother and my father. That seems to be very popular in the Caribbean. . . I knew my father but we were never very close.

Despite many of the officers growing up without a father, and despite the acknowledgement of the dual role played by their own, as well as many other mothers within Caribbean society, it was difficult for those interviewed to see beyond the maternal responsibilities of women. In the view of the participants, although women were forced to assume the role of provider when men refused or were unable to do so, their natural role remained that of nurturer and caregiver for their children.

Among the store owners/proprietors and police officers therefore, patriarchal assumptions about male and female suitability for various roles led to value judgements being made as to the relative importance of men and women, to the functioning of the family unit, with the care of children emerging as paramount. The implications of this are seen, where there is reluctance to take any action against women – seen as essential to the development of children – that may see them removed from the home. Men, by virtue of the expectation that they will not play as integral a role in their children's lives, are seen as more expendable by comparison.

Perceptions about male offending motivations

The gender role perceptions discussed earlier have direct implications for further assumptions made about the motivations to offend among male perpetrators. Participants made a number of assumptions about the offending of men that appeared to be related to their perceived lack of involvement in the lives of their children. As a result, there was very little compassion evident in discussions about male offending among shop owners/proprietors or the police. Beliefs were centred around the agency that was presumed to govern the actions of men who were unencumbered by familial responsibilities. Consequently, in the minds of participants, male offending was a choice rooted in self-serving motivations. Possible motivations suggested by shop owners/proprietors included the desire to get money through the sale of stolen goods, or trying to take advantage of store owners. Hassan, a 52-year-old owner of a small clothing store, explained:

> Men steal to prove a point, to get something over on you . . . a lot of men out there are able to work but choose not to. . . men don't steal for survival, they steal more for profit or for reasons of gain.

The notion of agency and choice is critical to an understanding of the manner in which male offending was viewed among participants when juxtaposed with perceptions of the motivations among women who shoplift. It was presumed that men were making the choice to steal despite alternatives available to them. While poverty was not unique to women, because of their responsibilities as mothers, it was believed that being poor impacted upon them in a unique and debilitating way. When women were poor it was more likely that her children would suffer the effects. In contrast to men therefore, when a woman did steal, it was generally for a good reason. This sentiment was captured in the words of Richard, a 37-year-old grocery store manager:

> You see a woman with two or three children, has no job, no father figure to help or take care of the kids and she has to provide for them. So, she goes into a store and shoplifts something which she hopes she can sell to get some money . . . You can sympathise with her. To me, a mother feels more pain and hurt to know that her children are hungry or don't have any clothes . . . Men don't care.

Jason, a 26-year-old police officer, shared similar sentiments:

> There are children that need to be taken care of . . . If a man and woman live in a household, you will find that the woman will take care of certain roles. The father may support the mother, but she is more likely to stay home with the children. He could go and wash cars, he could help someone lift up boxes, but a woman may have a child at home and not be able to feed him, so she may go steal.

Indeed, among the police officers interviewed, there was a reluctance to accept that a lack of legitimate opportunities for success may contribute to male offending. Men were characterised as lazy, and unwilling to take certain jobs, preferring instead to steal. Marcia, a 28-year-old officer, argued:

> In my career, the men that I see shoplifting can go and work. If a man feels that he needs fifty dollars. Week to support his family,

he would prefer to work for nothing that to work for twenty-five dollars . . . Men may not have any money. They aren't going to go and cut cane, but they will lime [be idle] all week and then go and rob somebody.

The testimony of the police and shop owners/proprietors demonstrated the privileging of the role of nurturer and caregiver, in that this appeared to be the only motivation that garnered sympathy. Traditional gender role perceptions had led to the assumption that this was almost exclusively the domain of women. The result of this was a situation in which it was difficult to accept that men would offend for this reason.

Police and civil society responses

Although anecdotal evidence has long suggested the existence of class bias among regional police forces, the issue of police bias has remained a virtually unexplored phenomenon within the Caribbean context. It has however received considerable attention in the United States, particularly against the background of racial bias following the fatal shooting of Michael Brown in Ferguson in 2014. Since then, the US policing profession has been facing what has been referred to as a 'crisis of legitimacy' (Nix, Campbell, Byers, & Alpert, 2017). There has been an acceptance both within the academic literature and among some in the law enforcement community itself that the actions and decisions of police officers are indeed at times affected by biases. Of particular concern have been racial disparities in the use of force by police officers against citizens. Studies have found that black US residents are three to four times more likely to have force used against them, and three times more likely to perceive that excessive force was used against them than white residents (Motley & Joe, 2018). Similarly, Fryer (2016) found that black New York residents were more likely than their white counterparts to experience a range of aggressive police interactions including use of hands (17% more likely), being pushed into walls or the ground (18% more likely) or having guns pointed at them (24% more likely). Research has also investigated the manifestations of racial bias in specific situations such as traffic stops (Epp, Maynard-Moody, & Haider-Markel, 2016; Horace & Rohlin, 2016; Ridgeway, 2006), pedestrian stops (Goel, Rao, & Shroff, 2016) and arrests (Lynch, Omori, Roussell, & Valasik, 2013), with general agreement that there are implicit racial biases in US policing.

Implicit biases are primarily subconscious or semiconscious perceptions and attitudes that guide behaviour (Dasgupta, 2013). There is debate, however, as to the nature of these biases. James (2018) provided a useful summary of the implications for policy of stable versus variable implicit biases. If biases are stable, and resistant to change, then efforts to alter these biases through education and sensitisation may be futile (Wilson, Lindsey, & Schooler, 2000). However, if these biases are variable, then it is possible that with time, there can be changes in attitude and associated behaviour (Plant & Peruche, 2005). Within the Caribbean, as discussed in Chapter 2, there exist patriarchal perceptions and assumptions that influence societal behaviour. The preceding narratives in this chapter support this existence among citizens in the form of shop owners/proprietors, as well as the police. There is evidence to suggest that even before offenders come into contact with the justice system, as a result of these assumptions, there are opportunities for them to be filtered out that are generally not afforded to men.

There is a perception problem faced by men who make the decision to steal. Shoplifting appeared to be a regular occurrence among the business operators. However, despite the acknowledgement that there was equal involvement of men and women, and despite the general belief that there had been a recent and dramatic increase in the number of women engaging in theft, gendered perceptions related to the offending motivations of perpetrators heavily influenced the actions of interview participants. Nowhere was this evidenced more so than in the expressed reluctance to afford male offenders the opportunity to explain themselves. Among shop owners/proprietors, there was a general practice whereby shoplifters, upon apprehension, were questioned privately as to what motivated them to steal. It is during this process that gender-based assumptions are either confirmed, or disproven, and the decision is made as to whether or not to call the police. All but one interview participant indicated the use of this practice. Richard provided context:

> You don't just want to call the police right away. Who knows? They might have something to tell me that would make me feel sorry for them and not press charges.

In reality however, the consequence of implicit biases among shop owners/proprietors was that this was a courtesy that was rarely extended to men. The testimony of participants demonstrated how preconceived notions about the offending motivations of men meant that there was very little that one could say that would alter existing perceptions. The characterisation of the male offender as strong and able-bodied, likely to not be burdened by familial responsibilities, making the decision to steal, contrasted unfavourably with the woman, forced into crime as a result of difficult life circumstances exacerbated by child care. The thoughts of Graham, a 56-year-old manager of a pharmacy, were in keeping with the general tone of those interviewed:

> I've never brought a man in here [for questioning]. For what? . . . He could go and wash cars, he could help somebody lift up boxes. But a woman may have a child at home and not be able to feed him.

Similarly, Hassan's encounter with a woman who attempted to steal was revealing:

> I felt sorry for her. I tried to put myself in her position. . .If she is stealing to feed her children, then it tugs on my heart. . .With women you need to find out . . . maybe she has a child . . . maybe she has a problem. . . may turn out to have three or four children and no husband to support them.

As a result, when faced with an incident of shoplifting involving a male offender, shop owners/proprietors are more likely to call the police than for a female perpetrator.

It is evident therefore that individuals are making discretionary choices based on gendered perceptions relating to male and female familial roles and specifically, their child care responsibilities. Despite the existence of laws and regulations designed to limit the application of bias to decision making among the police, it is inevitable that police officers too, at times, are forced to operate in spaces in which the use of their judgement is necessary. Although the police are expected to apply the law in a fair and just manner, the nature of their job means that there is often uncertainty surrounding the exact motivations for their actions, since their decisions are based largely on their own individual interpretations. Brown (1981) saw as the consequence of this the narrowing of the gap between written and actual law.

The application of bias takes place at all levels of the police hierarchy. Of particular relevance to the present study however are the offender variables, among which gender assumes particular significance, which may influence front line officers who have the power to apply laws and enforce punishments at the time of apprehension (Gaines & Glensor, 2004). Members of the RBPF who participated in the focus groups were asked about the use of discretion in the performance of their professional duties. Generally, participants saw this as an inevitable part of policing. Rodney, a 32-year old officer, provided his thoughts:

> Personal discretion is a big part of life within the force, in terms of how to deal with matters out there. We are supposed to be here to protect the public . . . Sometimes if you talk to someone, you achieve more than sending them to court.

This becomes problematic however when police discretion is guided by individual biases. Schafer and Mastrofski (2005) argued that there are justifications for the use of discretion that officers are comfortable admitting to such as a desire for increased efficacy. There are however other explanations that may be rooted in an affinity for one group over another. Among these are offender variables such as gender. Jason explained the manner in which male offenders are disadvantaged by the assumptions made about their familial roles:

> Women tend to steal to help their families. That is my experience. So, you might have a woman stealing some items, or some food because she doesn't have any choice, or she thinks she doesn't have a choice. What is the use of locking her up? . . . in many cases it may cause more harm than good to put that person before the court, than to simply talk to them and explain to them what they have done wrong. They may be more likely not to do it again if you deal with it that way.

Mark, a 43-year old officer, saw the unequal application of the law due to gender as a natural course of action:

> It's not just officers. I'm sure you, as a father, will treat your son differently from your daughter . . . You will have certain biases because we are human and that is how we are made up. . . Are you going to leave those children unattended for a period of time . . . ?

The testimony of Jason and Mark, indicative of the group, demonstrated the inexorable societal link between women and their familial functions in the home. Police officers are not insulated from cultural perceptions but rather are subject to the same values and beliefs. It is clear from these narratives that the officers believed that the well-being of children was tied to their mothers, and as such it was their removal from the home, and not that of men, that would prove detrimental.

Summary

Testimony from shop owners/proprietors and the police demonstrates that men appear to be affected negatively by a form of intervention that is influenced by gendered assumptions related to traditional roles in the home. These assumptions, in turn, influence perceptions held by civil society as to the motives for offending among male shoplifters as well as the availability to them, of perceived viable alternatives (unlike women). Focus groups with members of the RBPF further demonstrate that these gendered assumptions influence their daily interactions with male offenders. Since the welfare of children is of primary concern, and this is believed to be the domain of women, there is the assumption that the arrest and possible incarceration of men would not prove detrimental to child development. As a result, it appears that men are not afforded the opportunity to be filtered out before they come into contact with the justice system.

Note

1 The RBPF does not disaggregate statistics for theft from shops/stores (shoplifting) by sex in their statistical reports.

5 Gendered decision making in the courts

In this chapter I analyse the gendered treatment of male offenders by officials of the court using Steffensmeier's focal concerns theory as a frame of reference. Investigations into focal concerns have generally relied on a quantitative analysis of sentencing outcomes. Very few studies have sought to investigate the nature of the perceptions and stereotypes held by decision makers that govern these outcomes. I draw upon testimony from magistrates that would generally preside over cases of shoplifting and/or drug smuggling. The magistrates confirmed the importance that is placed on the role of maintaining and protecting family life – particularly as it relates to child rearing. This is a role that they assume is generally not played by Caribbean men. I analyse the extent to which these factors are taken into consideration at the time of sentencing. I examine the gendered decisions made by officers of the court and argue that because of the perceived lack of child rearing responsibilities many male offenders are not afforded the benefit of the doubt, when compared to women, when they come before the courts.

Two judicial levels operate within the Barbados justice system. At one level are the Magistrate Courts, while the second level consists of the Supreme Court (further divided into the High Court, and the Court of Appeal). The Magistrate Courts preside over civil, family and criminal matters. Semi-structured interviews were held with 9 of the 11 magistrates that were employed at the time of data collection.

Culture's influence on the law

There is a temptation to view the law, as operating within a vacuum, unaffected by outside influences. We assume that those charged with upholding the law make decisions independent of culture and are somewhat insulated from its effects. The law is more easily digested when viewed in this manner, and most conceptualisations of culture do not include the law in any significant way. In reality however, it would be illogical to attempt to separate social practices from the laws that govern them, or by extension from those employed to dispense justice. The relationship between the law and culture is a dynamic and interactive one, in that the law produces culture, as well as operating as one aspect of it (Mezey, 2001). Rosen (2006, p. xii) argued:

> Law is so deeply embedded in the particularities of each culture that carving it out as a separate domain and only later making note of its cultural connections distorts the nature of both law and culture.

Mezey discussed what she referred to as the pervasive power of culture and a legal realm that cannot be analysed without using culture as an essential variable. In explaining this power, she used the example of a culture of policing in the United States that saw African American drivers stopped at a higher rate than white drivers. The cultural practice of targeting minority drivers, despite the Equal Protection Clause's stipulation that race should not influence protection from unreasonable searches and seizures, is protected by law which has made the challenge of this practice in court virtually impossible. In this way the law serves as a vehicle through which dangerous cultural practices are reinforced (Mezey, 2001).

Similarly, within the Caribbean context, judicial decision makers are heavily influenced by patriarchal messages transmitted to them during childhood. In Chapter 3 I discussed socialisation mechanisms that influence the gender perceptions of Caribbean children. The narratives of the shop owners/proprietors and police in Chapter 4 illustrated the assimilation of these messages and the role that their home environment played in shaping their current perceptions of familial roles. This too was the background against which the magistrates interviewed were raised. When asked to describe the delineation of roles within their households as children, those who were raised by both parents described a traditionally gendered division of labour whereby mothers assumed domestic responsibilities while fathers were expected to provide for the family's financial needs[1]:

Patriarchal ideologies are internalised at a young age not only through the observation of parental roles but also through the comparative subordination of girls in the home in a manner that emphasises the domestic role that they are expected to play as adults (Mishra, Behera, & Babu, 2012). The childhood experience of a 60-year-old magistrate, Mr McDonald was typical of the socialisation practices within the households of the magistrates interviewed:

> I had to do chores like maintaining the animals we kept. My sister would mostly do the housework. My sister had to learn to cook because my mother thought it was a priority for her to learn to cook. It was not a priority for me to cook, although she would casually tell me I should learn, she never really enforced that.

Fifty-three-year-old Ms Jacobs, the only woman interviewed among the magistrates, shared a similar childhood experience with the men:

> My parents' roles were different. Although both worked, my father was clearly the breadwinner of the family. At home he did stuff outside. He wouldn't even iron his clothes. My mother did all the cooking and domestic responsibilities. As girls we would help with washing and cleaning. My father was very good at barking orders, but my mother was very nurturing. She was very lovey-lovey with us.

Given these socialising experiences, it is unsurprising that the magistrates interviewed would have grown to privilege the domestic responsibilities of women, and in particular their maternal functions over all other responsibilities. Patriarchal relations dictate that for women, their role as mothers becomes a central and defining feature of their existence. As a result, these messages, internalised as children, have a significant influence on the manner in which the magistrates view family relations as adults:

> . . . mothers just have this ability with children that men don't have. Obviously I'm not saying that men can't take care of children. But there's no doubt that in the early years of development the role of the mother is more important. There's no getting away from that. As I grew up and started my own family I took cues from how my parents did it. It worked with them and having those clearly defined responsibilities has worked for me too. I believe that children really need their mothers because in Barbados, to my mind, and maybe this is my own socialization, the children gravitate towards the mother more so than men in our society.
>
> (Mr. McDonald)

It is inevitable therefore that these patriarchal ideologies provide the context within which magistrates assess and treat the offending behaviour of male and female defendants.

Bounded rationality as a precursor to focal concerns

Herbert Simon (1955), in attempting to construct a theory of human economic behaviour, offered bounded rationality as a critique of existing economic theory, and in particular, the traditional depictions of rationality. Simon believed that rationality and behaviour were linked by the choice an individual makes among a range of alternatives, and that every behaviour was governed by such a choice (Barros, 2010). He argued that there was a lack of realism associated with the assumptions inherent in contemporary beliefs about rationality. These involved three steps: (1) knowledge of all behavioural alternatives; (2) full knowledge and anticipation of the possible consequences of each alternative; and (3) a predicted valuation of each consequence. Indeed, Simon believed that the very development of his theory of bounded rationality was justified by the manner in which it highlighted the 'practical impossibility' of these assumptions.

> ... the rationality of neoclassical theory, assumes that the decision maker has a comprehensive, consistent utility function, knows all the alternatives that are available for choice, can compute the expected value of utility associated with each alternative, and chooses the alternative that maximizes expected utility. Bounded rationality, a rationality that is consistent with our knowledge of actual human choice behavior, assumes that the decision maker must search for alternatives, has egregiously incomplete and inaccurate knowledge about the consequences of actions, and chooses actions that are expected to be satisfactory (attain targets while satisfying constraints).
>
> (Simon, 1997, p. 17)

Simon, rather than privileging the effect of external constraints on decision making, as was customary with traditional depictions of rationality, called for a recognition of the critical role played by internal constraints. Bounded rationality argues that individuals are limited by the boundaries of their thinking and the information available to them. Instead of maximising their benefit from a particular course of action, individuals search for acceptable alternatives according to pre-established criteria (Barros, 2010). Simon's central belief was that the 'inner environment' of a decision maker becomes active when the difficulty associated with a particular task exceeds the necessary threshold. This difficulty derives not only from an inability to gain access to all the information required, or a lack of knowledge, but also the incapability of the human mind to process it even if that were possible. As a reaction to this, the brain operates within the confines of its cognitive limits, or the 'psychological properties' of the individual (Simon, 1997).

Albonetti (1986) applied Simon's economic theory to human behaviour as it relates to courtroom decision making. Traditional rationality when applied to this scenario sees outcomes as solely dependent on relevant legal factors such as the nature of the crime committed, or the potential danger the offender may prove to society if released. Since there are specific rules that govern these factors, extra-legal considerations such as socio-economic status, gender and race/ethnicity should have no influence on sentencing. Conversely, the application of bounded rationality sees courtroom decision makers base their sentencing decisions partly on perceptions and stereotypes regarding the offender. According to this theory, judges and attorneys use a combination of legal and extra-legal considerations to arrive at sentences they deem to be appropriate. Albonetti found support for bounded rationality among his sample of prosecuting attorneys who in making screening decisions navigated their inevitable uncertainty through the use of extra-legal variables such as cooperation and/or credibility.

The theory of focal concerns

It is from this conceptualisation of bounded rationality that the theory of focal concerns emerged as a means of explaining judicial decision making, and in particular the motivations behind sentencing disparities. The theory is based on the assumption that in addition to operating under considerable time constraints, judges typically possess limited information about the defendant's culpability. In response to these deficiencies, they develop what has been referred to as perceptual shorthand, which is applied based on assumptions and stereotypes that they hold with regard to defendants that come before them in court (Hawkins, 1981). Steffensmeier's (1980a) original theorising of focal concerns involved the identification of five factors that, due to inadequate information, influence the decision making of judges as it relates to sentencing: (1) permanence of behaviour, (2) perception of dangerousness, (3) practicality, (4) chivalry and (5) naivete. Later however, Steffensmeier reorganised focal concerns theory around three central issues that were believed to be of primary concern to judges: (1) blameworthiness/culpability, (2) the desire to protect the community and (3) practical constraints and consequences (Steffensmeier, Kramer, & Streifel, 1993). Blameworthiness assesses the role that the offender played in the crime, the level of remorse shown by the offender and the nature of harm to the victim. The more blameworthy an offender is, the more likely he/she is to be treated harshly. Community protection reflects a desire to shield the community from future harm at the hands of the offender. This requires a determination of the seriousness of the offense and, how likely he/she is to re-offend if released. Finally, practical constraints consider the negative consequences of sentencing on the individual, as well as on the organisational capacity of the justice system. This involves a consideration of structural factors such as case backlog, prison overcrowding and maintaining productive relationships among prosecutors and defense attorneys. It also involves an assessment of the social costs such as the likelihood of job loss, offender special needs, the offender's familial responsibilities (does the offender have children; is he/she the sole caregiver) as well as those to the wider community (Rodriguez, Curry, & Lee, 2006).

Perceptual shorthand assists judges in making sense of offender behaviour and explains the process by which focal concerns produces sentencing disparities. It is governed by individual assumptions and stereotypes that may be linked to a range of factors including race, age and economic status. Indeed, research has generally agreed that such disparities are affected by the perceptions of courtroom decision makers (Harris, 2008; Kramer & Ulmer, 2006; Spohn, Beichner, & Davis-Frenzel, 2001). Defendants whose characteristics are in keeping with negative stereotypes concerning for example, their level of dangerousness or their likely ties to children and families are likely to receive harsher punishment (Ulmer & Johnson, 2004). Focal concerns are however a particularly useful theoretical lens with which to analyse the impact of gender on sentencing decisions with empirical data supporting the notion that disparities in sentencing among men and women can be explained against this background (Hartley, Maddan, & Spohn, 2007; Lin, Grattet, & Petersilia, 2010; Steffensmeier & Demuth, 2006). While it is clear that there is a link between each of the three central issues, identified by Steffensmeier, and offender gender, of particular concern to the present study is the gendered consideration of practical constraints by courtroom decision makers – specifically the social costs of incarceration, in the form of the possible disruption of the family unit, with children of paramount concern.

In Chapter 2, I discussed the notion of familial-based justice and the manner in which the sentencing decisions of judges are impacted by an offender's family status. Of critical consideration is the protection of children, with judges reluctant to remove those from the home that provide a caretaking role, particularly as it relates to emotional support (Steffensmeier, 1980b). In doing so, judges exercise a responsibility that in their view aims to ensure that decisions made in the courtroom do not have indirect negative consequences for the most vulnerable. Participants were asked to explain the perceived obligation that they felt as magistrates to the wider society. Mr Joseph, a 42-year-old magistrate, expanded:

> I feel that as an officer of the court, I have an obligation to protect children. Because there is a myth that we just lock up people, but there is wider responsibility. The child is really important. All the persons around the child that may have an impact, we have to address it. The consequences of hastily removing the parent from the home is that we will repeat the cycle of dysfunctional families. So, if a chance can be given to the parent, we can ultimately impact the child in a positive way.

The rapid growth of the United States prison population since the 1980s has provided researchers with the perfect opportunity to investigate the effects of parental incarceration on children – a reality for a large number of American children, particularly those of African American heritage (Lee, McCormick, Hicken, & Wildeman, 2015; Wakefield & Wildeman, 2018). Generally, the importance of continued parental presence for child development is well established in the literature (Collins, Maccoby, Steinberg, Hetherington, & Bornstein, 2000). It is important to note that children at risk for parental incarceration are likely to have been raised in conditions of socio-economic disadvantage. The experience of parental incarceration for many children therefore has the effect of compounding existing material deprivation. Evidence suggests that such children are at risk for a range of negative structural effects including poverty, homelessness, reduced access to educational opportunities and dependence on public assistance (Schwartz-Soicher, Geller, & Garfinkel, 2011; Sugie, 2012). In addition, parental incarceration has been found to place children at considerable short- and long-term risk of adverse development, with depression, anxiety, aggression and future criminal involvement the more common manifestations (Huebner & Gustafson, 2007; Murray, Loeber, & Pardini, 2012; Wakefield & Wildeman, 2018).

Although there is some disagreement in the literature as to the comparative effects of maternal and paternal incarceration, considerable evidence points to more negative outcomes resulting from the incarceration of mothers. Mothers have been found to be nearly three times as likely to have been engaged in sole caregiving responsibilities prior to incarceration than fathers (Glaze & Maruschack, 2008). When fathers go to prison therefore, caregiving responsibilities are likely to remain undisturbed, as opposed to the disruption of care arrangements that follow the arrest and Imprisonment of mothers (Murray & Murray, 2010). It has been argued that incarceration enforced mother-child separation significantly disrupts childhood development, especially in infancy, so much so that the negative impacts have been termed as 'enduring trauma' (Phillips & Harm, 1998). As a result, imprisoned mothers tend to report a greater escalation of problem behaviour among children than imprisoned fathers (Sroufe & Causadias, 2012).

Barrow (1996) argued that although stable conjugal relationships existed, the economic marginalisation of men had become a feature of Caribbean matrifocality. This sentiment has been echoed by more recent scholarship in the area that has suggested that for large numbers of Caribbean men, a lack of economic opportunity and the resulting limited earning potential have severely restricted their ability to contribute meaningfully to the emotional and economic well-being of the family (Quinlan & Flinn, 2005). This has led to a steady rise in the number of women operating as sole caregivers for children, and indeed the number of single-parent families in Barbados and the wider Caribbean (Reynolds, 2009). This reality, together with the expressed obligation to ensure the protection of children, leaves little doubt that magistrates take seriously the possible detrimental effects of removing a parent from the home. In the event that an offender is the sole caregiver, incarceration may result in children being placed in the care of neighbours, relatives or possibly the State (Raeder, 1993). The consideration of these practical concerns means therefore that offenders who are caring for children are less likely to be incarcerated than those who are not (Freiburger, 2010, 2011). In Chapter 2 I argued that although this premise of familial paternalism suggests that the removal of familied men should be deemed no less detrimental to the welfare of children than the removal of familied women, research has demonstrated this not to be the case (Daly, 1987; Simon and Ahn-Redding, 2005). Gendered disparities in sentencing result from the influence on sentencing outcomes, of personal biases, assumptions and beliefs about the respective familial roles of men and women, on the part of courtroom decision makers. The accounts of the magistrates interviewed illustrated the common belief that caregiving was the domain of women, and as such it was their presence, and not that of men who may offer only financial assistance, that was crucial. Mr Davis, a 39-year-old magistrate, provided his thoughts:

> . . . women obviously are the ones that do most of the nurturing. So the mothers principally who appear before me, are really the ones running the households. In the case of the men, they are not the ones in the household a lot. Maybe they are the main source of finance, but that's about it.

Ms Jacobs agreed:

> I am not going to say men don't take care of their families you know. Or that none of them play an important role. But as far as being there for children day in and day out. Taking care of everyone and everything in the house. We are the ones that do it. That's just how we were raised. If we aren't there children will feel it.

Gendered decision making in the courts

There is widespread agreement within the literature on sentencing, that sentencing disparity should occur on the basis of two main criteria – the seriousness of the crime and the dangerousness of the offender (Hamilton, 2017; Hofer, Blackwell, & Ruback, 1999). Unwarranted disparity arises where offenders are treated differently based on legally impermissible factors such as race, although many believe that differential treatment based on any extra-legal factor is unfair and unwarranted since it may be governed by conscious or subconscious bias towards particular groups (Hofer, Blackwell & Ruback, 1999). At the heart of this debate lies the issue of judicial discretion, and the level of autonomy that should be afforded to judges at the time of sentencing. The central issue here is the relative importance that should be given to judicial intuition, as opposed to formal guidelines external to the decision maker.

Fuelling this debate are two competing schools of thought. The first advocates for limited autonomy, arguing that judges should operate within the confines of a set of strict rules and principles that inform their sentencing decisions so as to remove the need for the use of discretion. In 1984, against the background of perceived misconduct on the part of judges, the United States, as part of the Sentencing Reform Act (SRA), adopted the federal Sentencing Guidelines. The guidelines had three main objectives: (1) to reduce the propensity for disparity in sentencing for similar offenders, (2) to ensure honesty in sentencing and (3) to ensure proportionality in sentencing (Brashear-Tiede, 2009). Judges were given a range of possible sentences that corresponded with the offense type, offense level and the offender's criminal history. It was hoped that this would achieve uniformity in sentencing and reduce the wide disparity that existed among different federal jurisdictions for similar offenses (USSC, 1987). In 2003 the United States Congress sought to further restrict judicial discretion as a result of what was viewed as increasingly arbitrary departures from the Guideline's mandates (Schanzenbach, 2005). The PROTECT Act/Feeney Amendment reduced the criteria for Guideline departures, and established monitoring mechanisms for judicial decisions. The act also gave attorneys the ability to report to congress any judge that in their opinion passed sentences that were in opposition to the Guidelines. Although data have demonstrated that there was a reduction in sentencing disparity post-Guidelines compared with pre-Guidelines (Brashear-Tiede, 2009; USSC, 2004), in 2005 the US Supreme Court ruled that the Guidelines were unconstitutional and ordered that they no longer be mandatory (United States v. Booker, 2005).

A second school of thought argues that although mandatory sentencing assists in achieving consistency, this comes at the expense of individualised justice. Sentencing Guidelines reduce decisions to formulas that can, as a result of a failure to acknowledge that the facts pertaining to every case are unique, produce unfair and unjust outcomes (Mallett, 2015). It posits that the context in which criminal offenses occur is important, and should be taken into consideration upon sentencing. Sentencing should be commensurate with the offense, the offender and the circumstances surrounding the specific crime. This process has been referred to as instinctive synthesis whereby there is a recognition that no definitive principles or rules can govern the treatment of every criminal offense. Instead judges intuitively assess all the factors relevant to a case in order to arrive at a sentencing decision (Anthony, Bartels, & Hopkins, 2016). This is a methodology in use in jurisdictions such as Canada and Australia. Indeed, Markarian v The Queen (2005, p. 51) described the process as:

> . . . the method of sentencing by which the judge identifies all the factors that are relevant to the sentence, discusses their significance and then makes a value judgment as to what is the appropriate sentence given all the factors of the case. Only at the end of the process does the judge determine the sentence.

The Barbados Penal System Reform (Amendment) Act (2014) is in keeping with this philosophy. The Act applies to those offenses for which sentencing is discretionary,[2] giving judges the autonomy to tailor sentences based on the specific circumstances of the case and the offender. Notwithstanding the recognised need for consistency in sentencing, the Act encourages the consideration of the possible mitigating factors that may have precipitated the offending behaviour, rather than adhering to a strict set of guidelines designed to limit discretion (Barbados Penal System Reform (Amendment) Act, 2014).[3] One of the aims of the Act was to advocate for the use of a range of alternatives to custodial sentencing that were available to judges. The principle of individualised justice holds that similar cases should be treated in a similar fashion; however, relevant differences should precipitate due allowance (Anthony, Bartels & Hopkins, 2016). The Barbados Penal Reform (Amendment) Act, by encouraging the consideration of relevant differences in the form of mitigating factors, widened the scope for the application of focal concerns by judges, leaving sentencing outcomes vulnerable to their biases and stereotypes.

Interviews demonstrated an inexorable link between these biases and stereotypes held by magistrates of the court relating to the respective familial roles played by men and women who have offended, and their proclivity to believe that men offend for any reason other than self-interest. The common depiction within the criminological literature of men who engage in acquisitive crime as being motivated by among other self-serving motivations, a desire to a secure masculine capital, was discussed in Chapter 2. In keeping with this, and the narratives of the shop owners and members of the Royal Barbados Police Force (RBPF) presented in Chapter 4, the magistrates interviewed made assumptions about the motivations of male offenders that were rooted in their own personal experiences as well as cultural stereotypes about the Caribbean family. A fifty-three-year-old magistrate Mr Smith explained:

> In Barbados, quite often, what I find disturbing is that for the most part when it comes to child rearing, you see females in the street . . . school time, shopping for children, in the church you see the mother, christening you see the mother. But you never ever see the father. And so, it follows that most mules for example, from my experience are females. Swallowers who are promised a sum of money by a male who disappears after they are caught. So most of the time it is money. Trying to get them and their children out of their economic rut. Saying they are going to do it once, and then

they get sucked in and do it more than once. Most of the time for the women it is out of need. For men it is more greed and ego. Who can manage the largest Cartel. Who can use brute force. Who can manipulate women to do their bidding.

Mr Brown too opined:

> The male offender is driven by a mixture of ego, driven by his desire not to be seen as weak by his peers, materialistic attainment. They are not generally driven by the more spiritual side of things. There are a lot of bravado and masculinity issues. Economic crimes are to keep up with what is seen in the movies and media. A heavy impact from America and a lesser impact from Jamaica. For female offenders they often don't know where the next meal is coming from and their children have needs.

The common view among the magistrates interviewed was that even in cohabiting relationships, it was women upon whom the responsibility for child care rested. It was women not men for whom the risks involved in engaging in criminal activity were worth it, in order to ensure that their children were taken care of. Children were the primary responsibility of mothers and as such this was the motivation that magistrates believed warranted consideration upon sentencing. It was not that magistrates were unwilling to afford lenient treatment to all male offenders. If the concern is for the welfare of children, then it follows that magistrates should deem the removal of familied men from the home as detrimental, particularly if they can prove sole care responsibilities. In Chapter 4, I discussed the manner in which store operators were reluctant to give male offenders the opportunity to explain their motives. While the legal framework provides this opportunity, primarily by way of a pre-sentencing report designed to supply magistrates with the information necessary to make an informed sentencing decision, as evidenced by the testimony of Mr McDonald, the gendered nature of focal concerns meant that for men, there was an insurmountable burn of proof:

> ... he [a male offender] would have a lot to do to convince me [that he is the sole provider for children]. Just because of how society is today I am less likely to believe that a man is committing crime to take care of his family as sole provider. I have had instances in which they come saying that they are supporting children and when I ask them to bring the mother, the mother says that she is receiving no support.

Since it was unlikely in their minds that the men that came before them played crucial and consistent roles in the lives of their children, participants were generally reluctant to see this as a possible motivation for their offending behaviour. As a result, magistrates did not see men as deserving of leniency. Almost unanimously participants made the assumption that the social costs to children, of removing men from the home, were minimal (as compared to removing mothers). The effect that this had on their decision making was apparent:

> It would be dishonest for me to say that my personal opinions don't affect my decisions. Sometimes you have an offender who is pleading guilty. I dig down to find out whether or not they have children, knowing that in single parent families, if you put away the mother it will be very, very difficult for the children. . . So you have two people charged for the same crime – a woman with children and a man with children. The mother tends to get a little lighter sentence. It's a sort of a little bias that comes out
>
> (Mr. McDonald)

Similarly, a 40-year-old magistrate, Mr Williams echoed similar sentiments:

> There's a high price for incarcerating mothers. I know that. A higher cost than incarcerating men. You would hardly find the type of caring gentleman involved with a female that goes to prison. Hence he is not the person to step up to the plate when she goes to prison. You would find it the other way around though. Where a woman would take care of children when the man is in prison. But when she is gone, children are left in the man's charge, and most time he is irresponsible. Many times they are left with a grandmother or aunt. The man doesn't assist in the real child rearing and instilling values. That plays a part in my decisions

Summary

In keeping with the findings presented in Chapter 4, the testimony of the magistrates interviewed suggests that in the Barbadian context, discretion is applied to the detriment of men as they come before the court. This is influenced by perceptions held about their comparative contributions to the overall development of their children. Familial paternalism places at the centre of judicial consideration the role that an offender plays in the lives of his/her children. There is indeed support, within the narratives presented in this chapter, for the notion that as a practical concern, the social costs associated with the incarceration of an offender, in the form of child care, are of primary concern to magistrates. Although women appear to be the main beneficiaries of this concern, it is important to recognise that this is rooted in a culture of patriarchal gender relations and as such does not represent evidence of a desire to protect women, as is often the assertion by those who advance the chivalry thesis. In reality, commonly ascribed conceptions of gender roles are integral to the manner in which the magistrates respond to male offending. The participants have assimilated cultural beliefs pertaining to men's familial roles and this is closely tied to assumptions made about their motivations to offend. So, when confronted with a male offender, magistrates act in ways that are commensurate with their patriarchal responsibility.

These are however limited representations of male offending, and do not take into consideration the nuance that may exist among the factors that encourage men to take part in criminal activity. Indeed, within the Caribbean context these assumptions are made in the absence of empirical support. The following chapter seeks to fill this void.

Notes

1 Single-parent households are the dominant form of Caribbean family (Blank, 2013; UNICEF, 2002). The majority of magistrates interviewed however were raised in households with both parents present.
2 The last crime to be made discretionary was that of murder by way of the Offenses Against the Person. (Amendment) Bill (2014) which changed the status of the sentence for murder from one fixed by a mandatory sentence to one that is discretionary in nature. All crimes are now discretionary.
3 The Barbados Penal System Reform (Amendment) Act (2014) recognised the following as 'mitigating factors': (a) the age of the offender, (b) the particular circumstances of the offender such as his social or economic circumstances, (c) whether the offender pleaded guilty and the point at which the guilty plea was made, (d) the circumstances or facts of the offense and the degree of the offender's involvement in offense and (e) any attempt by the offender to make reparation for the offense.

6 The voices of male offenders

Responses to poverty and threatened masculinity

The preceding chapters have discussed the assumptions made about male offending. I illustrated the role that these assumptions play in the treatment on male offenders by civil society and stakeholders within the justice system. In an effort to investigate the credibility of these assumptions, in this chapter I shift the discussion towards the voices of men incarcerated for drug smuggling. I argue that against the background of chronic deprivation, these men were searching for ways to reassert the masculinity that their poor economic status had prevented them from achieving through legitimate means. A desire to provide for themselves, the importance of being respected by others, and critically, despite assumptions to the contrary, for some, a need to support their families had made drug smuggling an attractive option.

Drug smuggling in the Caribbean

The two main substances trafficked through the Caribbean are cocaine and marijuana. Jamaica is the largest producer of marijuana in the region although exports appear to be in decline because of changes in market demand in receiving countries as well as more effective law enforcement in the region. In addition, the islands of the Caribbean provide the ideal location for the transhipment of cocaine from South America. In the 1980s, the Medellin Cartel used the island of Norman's Cay in the Bahamas in order to refuel planes destined for the United States. At the time, almost 75 per cent of cocaine seizures by the US government occurred in the Caribbean. Countries such as Jamaica and Trinidad and Tobago have also served as major entry and exit points, with cocaine seizures showing a dramatic rise in Trinidad after 2003. The islands, both in the Leeward and Windward groups, too experienced a dramatic increase in cocaine seizures between 2001 and 2004 with 60 per cent of all Caribbean cocaine seizures taking place in these islands in 2004 (UNODC; World Bank, 2007). This was followed by a period of decline with tougher law enforcement and a diversion to Central America and West Africa. The region is however experiencing a recent resurgence in use due to increased US investment in the war on drugs in Mexico and Central America (The Crime Report, 2018). There is also a political association and regular transport links with one of the major distribution centres in Europe – the Netherlands. Since drug smuggling by air requires adequate travel mechanisms in place, the good transport and migration networks between islands such as Suriname and the Dutch Caribbean islands have meant that these are attractive routes for the smuggling of cocaine produced in South America (Kloppenburg, 2013).

The trade in illegal drugs has become critical to the internal operations of Caribbean gangs as crime has become increasingly more organised. Indeed, the highest level of organisation is associated with those involved in the drug trade which has a tight hold over poor communities. Largely because of their involvement in the drug trade the gangs are now international, as they have criminal networks in Europe and North America. The case of Jamaica provides a useful example. Harriott (2003) identified several stages in the development of violent criminal activity in Jamaica, one of which involved the search for alternatives to legitimate activity. In developed countries technological change has both created and destroyed jobs, and one of the main problems is the distribution of the new jobs relative to that of the old. Developments in Jamaica over the past four decades have largely destroyed jobs, and the poor have borne the brunt of the onslaught. They endured not only the effects of the lack of economic opportunities but also the neglect of social services – education, health, housing – that was a part of the orthodoxy of the structural adjustment programme (Bissessar, 2013). While some middle-income workers, especially professionals in the financial sector that suffered job-loss, were able to use the legal migration option, this was not open to the unskilled. Instead, many young unskilled men were drawn into the drug trade:

> The young males whose illegal status, limited skills and acquisitive ambitions, coupled with a short time horizon for their fulfilment, made the opportunities in the American drug trade all too alluring.
> (Harriott, 2000, p. 8)

Residents of poor urban communities found alternatives therefore in the drug trade especially as it relates not only to the United States but also to Europe and other parts of the Caribbean. This served to transform the nature of Jamaican crime as firearms began to flood the country. Participants in Moser and Holland's (1997) study were unified in their belief that the violence within their communities became worse with the introduction of crack cocaine, since cocaine brought together the explosive combination of drugs and guns.

The majority of those apprehended at borders and ultimately incarcerated within the Caribbean for drug crimes are couriers, rather than the major players within the narcotics trade. Commonly referred to as 'mules' the tend to employ a variety of tactics aimed at avoiding detection. These include hiding drugs in suitcases, or on their person, as well as ingesting drug-filled pellets before boarding flights (Esmee Fairbairn Foundation, 2003). Drug mules are frequently detained at airports across the Caribbean. One of the more significant seizures occurred on 4 August 2011, when the Royal Barbados Police Force detained 20 persons arriving at Grantley Adams International Airport. Of this 20, ten were arrested after X-rays confirmed they had swallowed various quantities of drugs. A spokesman for the Police Force indicated that the influx of non-nationals attempting to bring illegal drugs into the country by any means had left them significantly concerned (Jamaica Observer, 2011).

Research into the motivations for drug smuggling has typically focused on female motivations, and has mirrored the gendered explanations for other forms of aquisitive crimes. Familial responsibilites and difficult life circumstances have been generally excluded from the possible motivations for male offending, and instead have been atrributed almost exclusively to women. Some have cited the emotional, physical and/or sexual abuse experienced by women from a young age, and the role that drug smuggling plays in attempting to mitigate these destructive long-term effects, either through their own poor decision making or as a result of coercion at the hands of exploitative male partners or family members (Fleetwood, 2015). Geiger (2006) found that adult victimisation in the form of poverty and abuse led to involvement in drug smuggling as a 'last expression of resistance' aimed at reclaiming a positive identity. Adler (1994) pointed to the effects of sole child care responsibilities among her sample of female couriers, and the manner in which this propelled struggling mothers into crime despite the threat of apprehension. Fleetwood (2015) too found familial pressures to be paramout in explanations for offending among Latin American smugglers, particularly as a reaction to pending crises such as debt repayment deadlines.

Although there exists a dearth of data specific to the Caribbean, BBC (2003) reported that for women, chronic poverty and the rewards of a successful trip were often factors too great to ignore. Although these women were making the conscious decision to participate, they were doing so as a result of the economic strain due to supporting a family on their own. One informant explained:

> "You could face the fact of being in prison – but then again, having four kids, working day and night, you're a mother on your own, you haven't got any father. Basically you just need a change – not only for yourself but for your kids."

> (BBC, 2003)

Poverty and crime

The contemporary economic realities within the Caribbean region necessitate the location of investigations into criminal motivations within the context of the conditions of poverty faced by large sectors of the population. Poverty has been found to have a variety of negative effects on individuals in response to, in particular, chronic conditions. These include a range of negative health outcomes, some attributed to the material deprivation associated with unemployment and others to the psychological stresses. In their study of teenagers in Britain, Warr, Banks, and Ullah (1985) found higher psychological distress figures among those who were poor. The majority of the symptoms were said to have started after a transition to unemployment. Many of the most serious symptoms occurred at about three months into unemployment. One study found that men who were poor were twice as likely to die than those who were not (Morris, Cook, & Shaper, 1994). Furthermore, they were more likely to commit suicide. Wilkinson (1996) believed that poverty can lead to a 'cycle of poor health' and an inability of an individual to be in total control of his life. He felt that, from the time of childhood, poor nutrition and the absence of a stimulating, positive environment can lead to health problems from which the child may never completely recover. Poor conditions, he felt, lead to poor health. As jobs become insecure, anxiety takes a toll on mental health and there is an increase in the incidence of depression and in self-reported ill-health (Burchell, 1994). But Cullen and Hodgetts (2001) presented poverty as an illness in itself. The social stigma and shame which often accompany poverty, they said, were similar to those associated with illness. Employment is an important part of 'normal' identity, while poverty and unemployment prevent people from feeling like normal functional members of society. So, the deprivation associated with these goes beyond the material to a deprivation of self-worth:

> Like a chronic illness, unemployment is not just something one suffers from; it requires one to renegotiate a sense of identity and to account for the appropriateness of one's strategies for bearing the affliction.
>
> (Cullen and Hodgetts, 2001, p. 41)

Classical theorists proposed a link between poverty and crime in that the poor were assumed to have different values which were responsible for their condition. This theme was taken up by the Chicago School, whose ecological approach allowed them to link areas of poverty with urban crime and other forms of deviance (Park, Burgess, & McKensie, 1928). On the one hand, they saw deviance as social constructions, but, on the other hand, as natural. In the ethnographic work of their students, there is a tentative move towards seeing the activities of the poor as attempts to negotiate structural constraints, a theme developed later by a number of social geographers. Oscar Lewis' culture of poverty thesis extended the notion of crime and the lifestyle of the poor as a cultural and intergenerational tendency to confront structural limitations (Lewis, 1965).

Thomas More, writing in the sixteenth century, suggested to his countrymen that there was little else for the poor to do than to go about 'a-begging' (Dickenson, 2000). Later writers were not as sympathetic as More appeared to be, preferring to adopt the individualistic theories that found favour in the nineteenth century. According to these theories, the poor were responsible for their condition in that they were either unable or unwilling to make adequate provisions for themselves. Booth, in his 1889 studies of poverty in London, distinguished a group within the ranks of the poor that formed a 'residuum' of criminal characters that was a blight on the rest of the poor (Alcock, 1997). One of the more persistent themes in the academic study of poverty and crime is its close association with unemployment. Unemployment poses several problems, the biggest and most immediate being financial. Gallie and Vogler (1994), in looking at the labour market in Britain, documented the kind of sacrifices that the unemployed are forced to make in order to make ends meet, such as the reduction of spending on necessary clothing and eventually on food. Notwithstanding the role of employment however, it is important to recognise that the negative effects of poverty are felt not only by the unemployed since for many, work does not provide adequate reprieve from their desperate circumstances. Indeed, the use of the word work by the middle and upper class can be seen as an affront to those who continue to suffer in low-paying, demeaning jobs (Young, 1999). For them, the notion of work as fulfilling is problematic. It was much more likely that these activities made crime and other illegitimate activities seem all the more attractive. Indeed, to Katz (1988), these activities could be seen as the 'seductions of crime'.

The link between poverty and crime has long been hotly debated, and a number of studies have been carried out to establish this link. The best support appears to come from micro-studies. From as far back as 1971, a longitudinal study of 399 18-year-olds in London showed that, for those who were poor, the rate of offending was about three times that for people who were not. Crimes for material gain were twice as likely to be committed when not working (Dickenson, 2000). This supports a view held by many today that poverty and unemployment lead to property crime since the poor would have something to gain in this instance. Others say that this is false as if a large number are poor, then there is very little to steal.

The question is: if poverty is related to levels of crime, why is it that young men rather than women appear to commit most of the crimes? This has been the subject of much debate from the nineteenth century, when, according to Carlen (Carlen, 1992), it was explained in biological terms. Women were seen as inherently passive and conservative, conditions engendered by the relative immobility of the ovule compared with the activity of the sperm. Pollack (1950) suggested that female criminality was masked because women are more deceitful, and they instigate rather than perpetrate, and because the police and courts are chivalrous, there is a tendency to be more lenient with women. Carlen (1992) believed that women are involved in more non-serious crime than reported, but that their involvement in serious offences is not under-reported. They may be less involved because of socialisation and social control, which often confine them to the home at an age when most of the crimes are likely to be committed. They therefore have fewer opportunities to commit crimes.

In looking specifically at the Caribbean situation, the anthropologist Penn Handwerker (1992) argued that women have different adaptive strategies, and he described the strategies in the context of resource access theory, a theory about what people do under particular circumstances. People, he said, are intelligent beings and use their imagination to understand their sensory environment. They generate a stream of conceptual innovations as they wrestle with the problem of understanding material stimuli and make choices consciously and unconsciously. In time, cultural and behavioural patterns emerge around ways of acting that improve access to resources. In poor families in the Caribbean, a woman's material welfare "was conditional on liens she held on men's wages. . ." (Handwerker, 1991, p. 1251). Men were gatekeepers and women resource seekers "with little to exchange for material support other than their sexuality and childbearing capacities" (Handwerker, 1991, p. 1252), for childbearing was essential to receiving help from men. Handwerker interpreted the fertility transition in Antigua and Barbados in terms of the structural changes in the economies of these islands, which allowed women to escape dependence on men and on childbearing. Levy (1996, p. 21), in the participatory rapid appraisal (PRA) of five inner-city communities, concluded:

> A boy must be tough so he turns to a gun. A girl can find a man to support her because she looks good. The link, therefore, between unemployment and crime and violence refers above all to men. For women without work the most common and preferred means of survival is dependence on a man.

As a result of the failure of Caribbean economies to provide adequate and sustained employment opportunities for the masses, large sectors of the populations are excluded from the workforce and although some work sporadically, unemployment has become the norm for them. The men in Bailey's (2010) study described moving in and out of the revolving door of short-term dead-end jobs in Jamaica. Many tried to make a living in the growing informal sector, but the activities in this sector are marginal, and where there is improvement in skills it comes from the entry of the better-off, who are engaged in multiple jobs.

Difficult life circumstances among male offenders

It was unsurprising therefore that poverty emerged as one of the main themes from the interviews. In Chapter 1 I discussed the high levels of poverty that have historically characterised much of the Caribbean. It is within these conditions that the men involved in this study lived most of their lives. Not only were these men currently living in conditions of poverty, but critically, there had been a chronic nature to their circumstances. Participants had generally been raised in conditions of significant deprivation and in keeping with contemporary regional indicators of poverty, they were typically raised in single-parent female-headed households. Bailey, Lashley and Barrow (2019) showed that as many as 48 per cent of poor households in Barbados are headed by women. The widening of the gap between men and women who live in poverty has been referred to as the feminisation of poverty as women, living alone, often charged with the sole care of children, demonstrate low labour force participation resulting in the greater likelihood that they will have no one employed in their household when compared to those headed by men (1998). With one study reporting that as many as 59 per cent of all children in the Caribbean are raised in single-parent female-headed households (UNICEF, 2002), it means that a significant proportion of children are vulnerable to conditions of poverty as women struggle to ensure both the economic and emotional well-being of their families. Lucien, a 25-year-old Jamaican inmate, described his situation:

> I was raised by my mother. It was seven of us, with no father. . . Things were never too pretty. I lived in the ghetto with poor water, light, no proper facility, no flush toilet. Everybody in the community was like that. We had to catch water somewhere. Sometimes we would burst the water main just to get water. . . I did not have three meals a day. In a day I would get a one pot for the day. Sometimes I wonder how she (mom) did it. She tried to go to school at the same time to get an education, so she had to leave early in the mornings. The bigger ones in the family had to take care of the little ones. She never had time for our education. If we missed school sometimes she didn't even know.

Lucien's experience reflected the general tone of the participants. Romario, a 30-year old from Guyana, was raised in similar circumstances:

> Boy, my mother was everything to us. Mother, father, everything. She had to be because I've never met my father in my life. She raised three boys on her own in a rough area. The community I grew up in was poor man, really poor. Crime, poverty. . . we didn't know where our next meal was coming from. And it wasn't just us. It seemed like everybody in the community was in the same situation. That was just life. But we managed to survive.

Sociologists have had widely differing views of the role of education in the society, but two issues emerge clearly from the debate. One concerns the role of education in the transmission of values and to some extent its transformative nature, while the other, more relevant to the present study, revolves around the question of inequality in access. Children in particular are at the mercy of circumstance and for them, access is synonymous with opportunity since unlike adults, they are unable to be proactive in obtaining basic needs. Children are not responsible for their economic circumstances despite the fact that this has significant implications for their long-term development (World Bank, 2006). It is generally accepted that education is an important vehicle with which to rise out of poverty. A number of poverty reduction strategies have cited education as being ". . . one of the most powerful instruments societies have for reducing deprivation and vulnerability . . . and affords the disadvantaged a voice in society and the political system" (World Bank, 2001, p. 2). Research has shown however that children of the poor have a lesser probability of accessing education than those of the middle and upper classes (Barros, Ferreira, Molinas, & Chanduvi, 2009; Molinas et al., 2010). When Halsey, Heath and Ridge (1980) looked at the key decisions, which defined the educational career of children, they found that the parents' material circumstances, which determined how long children could be kept in school, were key factors. For Caribbean children, despite academic education continuing to be the most effective means of upward mobility, education among the lower stratum has traditionally been dysfunctional (Boxill & Quarless, 2005). The inability to meet education costs as well as family pressure to assist in income generation forces large numbers of children to drop out of school (Bailey, 2004). Eddie, a 25-year-old inmate from Jamaica, explained his reasons for not finishing school:

Things were rough man. We weren't eating on a regular basis. I went up to second form. Then my father said it was time to get work. I needed to take on some of the load financially. We were all hungry. So, I left school early and started to work.

Similarly, 29-year-old Guyanese inmate, Devon lamented:

Some of my brothers and sisters were only able to do the first term of Grade seven. Our mother didn't have the money to pay school fees. I did grade seven at one school, then dropped out and picked up again at grade seven in another school. I wasn't able to finish high school though. We just didn't have the money to pay for everything. I wanted to play football and needed shoes, I needed uniform, I needed books. There just wasn't any money for any of it. So, I stopped going.

The marketisation of education has therefore effectively locked out the poor from the best that Caribbean societies have to offer, meaning that they are not competing on equal terms. Education serves to provide opportunities for higher level future employment and the associated upward social mobility. However, childhood experiences meant that the adult reality among these young men was an existence bereft of academic qualifications or vocational skills with little or no savings. When asked to describe their economic situation at the time of their incarceration, it was evident that for the majority of those interviewed, conditions had not improved. Romario provided insight:

> When I left home I rented an apartment. I am going to be thirty later this month and I've rented that apartment now for six years. The neighbourhood is poor but probably a bit better than where I came from. It was very difficult to get by, I have rent, I try to buy things for women. . . I have over GYD $100,000 in debt. I was self-employed. Cut grass, trees. I would go around with a weed whacker and see who wanted to hire me. The money was not a lot at all but I guess it paid me.

Romario's testimony was representative of the situation faced by the majority of those interviewed. A lack of education had rendered him helpless to improve his living conditions beyond what he had experienced as a child. For him, periods of unemployment were interrupted by occasional menial labour aimed at survival. As discussed in Chapter 2, Beth Ritchie's theory of gender entrapment examined womens' criminal involvement against the background of the 'chaos' caused by outside forces of which culturally expected gender roles as they relate to child care assume prominence. This chaos, in turn, combines with poverty to limit the choices available to women, and thus forces them into crime (Ritchie, 1996). Such theorising brings the issue of agency to the fore, as it depicts individuals as being vulnerable to uncontrollable forces beyond their control. Scholars have generally been unwilling to interpret male criminal responses to outside forces in this way. While some individuals do have the strength of character to escape from environmental constraints, there can be little doubt that circumstances can be so debilitating that the range of choices is constrained, and under conditions of multiple deprivation, life chances may be restricted by forces that test resolve. The testimonies here suggest that among a subset of male offenders living in desperate conditions, there exists a form of chaos too, at the base of which lies the interaction between poverty and masculinity. In some cases this leads to a constraining of choices in a manner similar to that described by Ritchie.

In Chapter 4 I discussed the notion of the male provider as being central to constructions of Caribbean masculinity despite this being an unattainable goal for a large proportion of men. The narratives of many of the inmates interviewed suggested that their decision to engage in crime was heavily influenced by an inability to achieve this goal, in the face of societal and personal pressures relating to their status as men. In the absence of legitimate avenues, the interaction between their chronic poverty and the desire to provide for their families, for a subset of participants, resulted in criminal involvement. Twenty-seven-year-old Barbadian, James explained the circumstances surrounding his decision to offend:

> I moved out on my own when I was twenty. I was doing gardening work and making a little bit of money. That was bad enough when I was living by myself but a few years later I moved in with my girlfriend. She had three children so over the years it put a big strain on us financially. We had trouble feeding the children and sending them to school. I needed money so badly. A friend of mine said he could help me out if I transported some drugs in my van. He said he knew some guys who did it. I thought about it. . .saw it as a way to pay off the debt and make things ok at home. He promised me BDS $10,000. The debt was BDS $12,000. I did it because of the pressures.

Thirty-two-year-old Vincentian Phillip too described the manner in which the struggle to financially support five children constrained his choices such that drug smuggling became an attractive solution:

> I lived with my girlfriend. I had a lot of responsibilities. She wasn't working. I had to maintain five kids – two mine and three hers. It was hard. I paid all the bills and had to make sure she had money in her pocket every week. After a while I couldn't find any work. Money was pretty tight. Nothing was coming in. A guy talked me into bringing some drugs for him from St Vincent to Barbados. I couldn't afford to wait until the children had no food. I really didn't want to do it. It was the only way.

While James and Phillip represented examples of offenders for whom child care responsibilities were cited as primary motivating factors, others demonstrated a desire to provide not only for children but also for their parents, and in particular mothers, to whom they felt considerable gratitude for past sacrifices. Lucien argued for example:

> Even though we were poor growing up my mother always did the best she could. She did so much for us. I always wanted to be able

to repay her. I never want to let her down. I just wanted to make her live nice and be happy. I really wanted to be able to help my mother. I still want to. I thought if I could just get enough money to get my mother a house so she has somewhere decent to live. . .

The preceding narratives depict motivations borne out of long-term financial hardships exacerbated by domestic responsibilities in the form of children or parents. Despite the persistent perception of men as primary providers in the home, Lewis (2004a) argued that global economic restructuring had left the Caribbean male in an economic and social crisis partly manifested in the dislocation of gender roles. At the heart of this was the destruction of the notion of the male breadwinner. In reality, the concept of the male breadwinner has been under pressure for some time, with some arguing that extreme stress arises when it becomes impossible for many Caribbean men to carry out that role (Connell, 1995).

Respect

There is a dynamic nature to expressions of masculinity which sees cultural variations by time and space. Within the context of deprived, urban, inner-city communities, demonstrating one's maleness is intrinsically linked to the notion of respect (Manninen, 2013). Barnett and Whiteside (2002) describe the urban ghetto as a 'noisy' place. In addition to the noise of the 'ghetto blasters' there is the 'noise' of the struggle of deprived men and women to survive under stress and in order to be heard, they have to shout. The exaggerated responses of those caught in this situation can be seen as efforts to communicate messages of worth (Bailey, Branche, McGarritty, & Stuart, 1998). They try to earn respect through a variety of means including their form of dress – clothes, flashy jewellery as well as violence. Because of the structural unavailability of educational, professional and employment status in marginalised communities, the evolution of distinctive behaviour patterns is inevitable. In-group behaviour patterns serve a variety of purposes, as, for example, rites of passage and declarations of personal identity within the group (Adams, 2007). Wallace, Fullilove and Flisher's (1996) study in Harlem, New York found that the demonstration of a willingness to commit violent acts was one way of ensuring personal safety. Any sign of weakness would signal to others that one was a 'punk', and punks could be victimised. Real men were left alone. This was one of the rules of personal safety in Harlem. This was a long-standing ritual, but the repercussions of being 'manly' changed with the introduction of guns that are more lethal than fists. The behaviour is employed as a:

> . . . code for the rapid communication of . . . personal statements and other information along the tightly self-interactive and geographically-focused social networks of oppressed and marginalized communities.
>
> (Wallace, Fullilove, & Flisher, 1996, p. 344)

Similarly, Bailey (2004) examined the mobilisation of physical strength among young unemployed men in Kingston's inner-city, as they struggled to survive in a subculture that revolved around masculine power and respect. This is the background from which many of the men in the present study emerged. Sammy, a 29-year-old inmate from Antigua, described his involvement in crime in these terms:

> This is life in the streets you know. People have guns, people get killed. I owned my first gun when I was fourteen. I shot someone for the first time when I was seventeen. Sometimes you might shoot someone cause him disrespect you. Respect is the most important thing in the ghetto. People look up to you because you are selling drugs. I even had people older than me looking up to me. A job came to me. A man offered me a lot of money to move some drugs to Barbados. I took it. They set me up though. When I get back home I will deal with them. . .I would prefer to live life legitimately but I don't have a chance. You go work as a labourer and barely make any money. I want to own a house, I want to own a car, have jewelry, the latest things. You need these things to get women, impress the girls. I have no regrets though. I get benefits from it. When I get out I will do it again. I'm willing to do this until I die.

Within poor communities therefore, where sources of respect are in short supply, crime becomes an important means of asserting one's masculinity through the respect it earns from peers. Poverty leads to feelings of powerlessness and frustration, where opportunities to demonstrate autonomy are severely limited. As a result, in an attempt to retrieve some sense of power and control, offending may occur (Connell & Messerschmidt, 2005).

Life in the streets involves a highly competitive performance of maleness among young men. This is where validation occurs and styles and attitudes are adopted to secure masculinity. In this sense, respect is garnered not only from behaviour but also from appearance, in that individuals begin to use goods to create their social 'self' and identity becomes constructed rather than revealed. In acquiring these goods, these men establish themselves with the meanings embedded in these goods. This is the ideology of consumerism described by Bocock (1993) and subsequently tied to emerging masculinities that have become embedded with appearance norms (Ricciardelli, 2011). Among poor men, this assumes special significance since respect from socio-economic status is non-existent. As a result, the acquisition and use of certain items – clothes, shoes, jewellery – becomes essential. The search for respect leads to actions not so much motivated by the desire to copy their 'betters', but to demonstrate style and be attractive to themselves and to others to make a statement. Young (1999) discussed the immersion of poor, black Americans in the ghetto in American culture, his discovery of their preoccupation with brand-name products and the extent to which they shared the values of the included. The styles of the American ghetto are the styles too of Caribbean inner-city youths. There is considerable pressure among young men to match the consumption patterns of the middle classes. Although unemployed, poor and marginalised, they are exposed to the messages and commodities from all over the world. The problem is that the virtual society set up by modern mass communication both includes and excludes both absorbs and rejects, and it is the blurring of the boundaries that explains the nature of the discontent at the bottom (Young, 1999). The urban ghetto therefore is the scene of the 'noise' of contest and conquest where the behavioural code is not only a means of demanding respect from male peers but also in order to attract the attention of women.

It was evident from the discussions that chronic conditions had led to a desire among some to compensate through a performance of masculinity. Romario explained:

> Me and my brother used to come together every day and smoke weed together; drink together. People used to like my style. I like that. I needed money to keep it up though. All the money I got I would use to buy clothes. I can't be looking like a nobody. I like to look clean. Nobody else was getting things for me so I had to get it for myself. I want to look good too you know! I see shoes and things and want to look good. I want to look good too you know!

Romario saw his appearance as representative of the image he wanted to portray to his peers. His involvement in crime therefore was seen as a way of maintaining this image and by extension, ensuring the continued respect of those around him.

Summary

The poverty faced by participants was a constant theme that ran through the various narratives. As discussed earlier, that such conditions may give rise to criminal involvement is well established in the literature. Poverty in and of itself however cannot predict offending. A more adequate prediction derives from an analysis of the responses to poverty, and responses are heavily influenced on the gender of an individual (Hay, 2003). The men in the present study were reacting to the threatened masculinity that resulted from living in conditions of chronic deprivation. This struggle manifested in two main ways. In the preceding chapters I have demonstrated the manner in which civil society and members of law enforcement have been guided by the gendered assumptions held regarding male and female motivations to offend. Contrary to prevailing beliefs, a number of the participants explained their involvement in drug smuggling in terms of providing not only for themselves but also for the wives, children and mothers to whom they felt obligated to provide for. There has been an empirical reluctance to depict male offenders in this way, or to interpret this intersection between gender and difficult life circumstances among male offenders as 'acceptable' causation as it relates to criminal involvement. Indeed, feminist and pro-feminist scholars have argued that the unique circumstances that combine to force women into crime are in stark contrast to the more self-serving motivations of men – so much so that some have called for the differential treatment of women versus men when they come before the courts (Katz, 2000; Radosh, 2002; Widom, 2000). The narratives presented in this chapter have however illustrated that stresses due to economic hardships are indeed not limited to women, thus necessitating a rethink of these exclusively linear representations.

The second manifestation of the struggle to reassert their masculinity however saw participants suggest motivations more in keeping with traditional depictions of male offending which centre on greed and economic gain. These motivations appeared to be incompatible with need and rather moved the discussion towards the achievement of a commodity critical to their status as men – respect. Although both sets of motivating factors are operating against the background of long-term conditions of poverty, it is perhaps this subset of male offender that gives some credence to the arguments of feminist scholars, as well as to the widely held gendered perceptions about offending behaviour.

7 Conclusion

In this final chapter I briefly synthesise the main findings of this study and in doing so present a theoretical frame against which further studies on the gendered treatment of offenders in the Caribbean can be based. I go on to discuss the notion of the absent father, which emerged as critical to the manner in which stakeholders themselves made sense of their own attitudes towards male offending. Finally, I end by discussing the findings against the background of the traditional undervaluing of the child care responsibilities traditionally ascribed to women.

It is important to note that, as with all qualitative research, the aim of this manuscript was not to present the data as representative of the views of all the stakeholders involved. Although there is often a temptation to view data as indisputable fact, the research that formed the basis of this manuscript was based on the views of a small number of shop owners/proprietors, police officers that would generally respond to reports of shoplifting, magistrates that typically preside over cases of shoplifting and/or drug smuggling and male offenders incarcerated for drug smuggling at Her Majesty's Prison. This manuscript, through an interrogation of the perceptions of these stakeholders, was aimed at contributing to the dearth of literature on the intersection between gender studies and criminology, and specifically the association between offender gender and the treatment of offenders in Barbados.

The data presented demonstrates that (1) in Barbados, decisions made by members of the judiciary, the police and general citizenry concerning criminal offenders are affected by cultural stereotypes specifically surrounding the care of children. The gendered assumptions held by shop owners/proprietors work to deny men the opportunity to be filtered out before they come into contact with the justice system. Once in contact, there is evidence to support theoretical perspectives that argue that, against the background of bounded rationality, judicial decision makers faced with inadequate information perceive discretion to be warranted (or not) on the basis of these assumptions. (2) These assumptions and stereotypes are guided by patriarchal relations, the nature of which mean that it is difficult to view men as being primarily responsible for the nurturing and care of children since this is seen as the domain of women. (3) These patriarchal stereotypes lead to assumptions about the criminal motivations of male offenders, often juxtaposed against assumptions made about those of women. Explanations for offending that garner sympathy among those interviewed almost exclusively centre around child care responsibilities. The belief that men do not play the essential caregiving role in the household is therefore incompatible with such motivations. As a consequence of this, when confronted with the case of a male offender, it is more conceivable that he has offended due to self-serving motivations such as greed and excitement, rendering him undeserving of sympathy and any associated leniency. And (4) as a result of these factors, it is not deemed to be detrimental to children to remove male offenders from the home and so little consideration appears to be given to preventing this occurrence.

The absent father?

This manuscript makes the point that the assumption that men are at best peripherally involved in child rearing responsibilities is due in part to the patriarchal belief that this is the domain of women. The offending motivations of men therefore are assumed to be self-serving while the motivations of women are in keeping with their domestic priorities. In Chapter 2 I discussed the binary representations of male and female offending that have found support within the criminological literature. The narratives of those interviewed for this study suggest an adherence too among stakeholders to these representations. In reality, the offender interviews illustrated the inadequacy of these portrayals, with explanations for male offending comprising a range of motivations, among which those borne out of greed form only a part. Chapter 6 explored the attempts by offenders to reassert the masculinity that had been under stress due to conditions of chronic poverty. While some responded to this struggle in ways consistent with the assumptions made by civil society and law enforcement, other offenders saw their involvement in crime as a means of providing for those whom they felt duty bound to support. Prominent among these were children.

Where sympathy is derived primarily from explanations rooted in child care, the apparent apathy typically felt towards the circumstances surrounding male offending is influenced by the belief that men are, in large part, absent from the lives of their children. The black male has long been depicted as one who may father children, but is reluctant to assume the role of father. He is seen by many to be a non-essential part of the family structure due in large part to the high percentage of black children raised in single-parent, households headed by women. Research has found that as many as 50 per cent of African American children are being raised in mother-only households (Coles & Green, 2010). Similar figures have been found among black families in Britain, and in the Caribbean (Reynolds, 2009). It would be misleading to ignore the reality that many black men are indeed uninvolved in the caregiving responsibilities associated with parenthood. The literature on fathering contains numerous accounts in the form of memoirs by men and women who relate their own experiences with, and the effects of being raised without the parental involvement of their fathers (Datcher, 2001; Pitts, 1999). Nevertheless, the term and notion of absence have been rightly identified as problematic due to its conflation with non-residence. Absence suggests invisibility, and this is, in many instances, an inaccurate portrayal of the parenting practices of black men (Coles & Green, 2010).

Much of what is known about the participation and fathering practices of black men has come from Caribbean scholarship (Barrow, 1996; Ricketts & Anderson, 2008) where non-resident fathers have long been a common feature of family life. As discussed in Chapter 3, the historical and cultural context is however essential to understanding these parenting practices and can be traced back to the institution of slavery. Within West African societies, marriage and childbearing were seen as cultural expectations with high value being placed on family relationships (Azevedo, 2011). Marriage did not operate within the confines of the nuclear family as is common in Western societies, but rather as an extended network which saw characteristics such as community and collectiveness as paramount. Indeed, the raising of children was seen as the responsibility of this extended network. Within this structure, parental roles were fluid and unrelated to gender although fathers were viewed as family heads. While women had a closer attachment to children, they were still expected to contribute economically through the production and sale of agricultural goods (Hill, 1999).

Slavery led to the decimation of African families as fathers were separated from wives and children, and taken to the Caribbean where many formed new relationships. Slaves valued marriage and so often remarried; however, new families were disrupted too by the fact that male slaves were frequently sold to new plantation owners, and forced to leave their children and wives behind. Poor records on families meant that the new emerging slave family was one which was female led, with the role of the father less clearly defined (Green, 2017). Although the process of post-slavery reconstitution saw many ex slaves attempt to find their families on other plantations, the institution of slavery damaged the West African family structure such that mating practices became characterised by casual sex, unstable unions and multiple associations. Slaves brought with them to the Caribbean values that stressed the importance of family, and kinship rooted in blood ties. Black men were therefore socialised to ensure that they recognised their caring roles for mothers, siblings and children as more important than those established through intimate relationships (Barrow, 1996). The groundwork for contemporary female-headed households as well as the role of fathers within the family structure was laid during this period in that although marriage remains important among black families today, blood ties take precedence (Reynolds, 2009).

Caribbean data on household composition reflect the manner in which black families have been affected by this colonial legacy. The case of Jamaica for example demonstrates the large number of contemporary households now headed by women. In 1996, roughly 40 per cent of all Jamaican households were headed by women (Bailey, Branche & Le Franc, 1998). This figure rose to 45 per cent in 2010 (Green, 2017). In Barbados, research has placed this figure as high as 48 per cent (Bailey, Lashley & Barrow, 2019). Against the background of these figures, there is a temptation to assume that non-residence automatically translates to non-involvement. Despite the belief, however, that black fathers more often than not make themselves unavailable to their children due to a lack of desire to take responsibility for them, there is evidence to suggest this to be overstated. Research investigating male parenting behaviour has traditionally conceptualised father involvement in terms of economic provision. However recently, studies have sought to include non-economic measures of involvement such as a father's influence on the cognitive, social and emotional development of his children (Cheadle, Amato, & King, 2010; Pleck & Masciadrelli, 2004). The inclusion of non-economic measures of involvement has emphasised the importance of elements such as engagement including activities such as changing diapers, giving advice or playing games; accessibility which relates to how available a father is when called upon; and responsibility which reflects the initiative shown by a father to tend to the general welfare of his child (Cheadle, Amato, & King, 2010). Indeed, non-economic measures of involvement have been found to more accurately reflect the parenting practices of many black fathers who appear to prioritise these activities over provider responsibilities (Cheadle, Amato, & King, 2010; Hamer, 2001).

The men interviewed in Reynolds' (2009) study of black fathers were aware of the negative stereotypes that surround their parental involvement. They rejected the characterisation of them as 'bad fathers' given to them due to their failure to adhere to the Western ideal that prescribes the role of economic provider to the father. Having been excluded from the processes that would see them able to fulfil this role, the fathers developed alternative methods of involvement that included spending time with their children, providing emotional support and acting as positive role models. Similarly, research has found that many non-resident Caribbean fathers play active and critical roles in the lives of their children. One study found that 87 per cent of non-resident Jamaican fathers reported that they were involved in their children's lives through various means including food provision, buying clothes and assisting with health care (Bailey, Branche, Jackson, & Lee, 2004). Other methods of involvement include spiritual guidance, facilitation of education and being 'friends' with their children (Anderson & Daley, 2015). The majority of men in Chevannes' (2001) Jamaican study reported that they played with their children, helped with homework, as well as assisted in domestic chores such as tidying up and cooking, although on a small scale, and with the belief that these were still duties inherent to women. Brown, Anderson and Chevannes (1993) argued that their most important finding was the strong commitment to fathering which united men of all classes and ages, "fathering is both part of a man's self-definition and his route to maturity" (Brown, Anderson, & Chevannes, 1993, p. 195). Caribbean research on fathering has, like mothering, been tied to sociological and anthropological studies on the Caribbean family structure. Nonetheless, this research provides meaningful points of analysis for feminist work. The 1993 Jamaican pilot study on the contribution of Caribbean men to the family indicated that the early 1980s plan to promote child development was challenged by the stereotypical assumptions of the 'absent' or 'irresponsible, uninvolved and interested' fathers (Brown, 1995). These beliefs that became platforms for many family and child development studies and policies began with a flawed assumption which led to the belief that intervention should be focused on getting fathers 'involved' in the family (Brown, Anderson & Chevannes, 1993).

The assumption that Caribbean men are absent from the lives of their children, though in many cases true, is one of several harmful gendered stereotypes that influence the decision making of civil society and law enforcement and can have considerable repercussions for families. This study revealed a deep-rooted concern among interview participants (civil society, police, magistrates) for the welfare of children. As discussed, the belief that it is women who do and should play the crucial role in the development and welfare of children has translated to actions that suggest that the incarceration of men will not have a significantly detrimental effect on their children. These actions however exist in the face of evidence to the contrary. Although the majority of research on parental incarceration focuses on incarcerated mothers, a growing body of literature speaks to the negative outcomes related to paternal incarceration. It is argued that while most non-resident fathers still maintain contact with their children, incarcerated fathers are much less likely to see their children on a regular basis (Hairston, 1998). As a result, the positive effects of direct father-child contact are eliminated with the removal of the father. Paternal incarceration has been found to lead to the financial instability of children leaving them vulnerable to the effects of poverty (Sugie, 2012), In addition, paternal incarceration has been associated with a range of mental health and behavioural problems such as poor school performance, depression, anxiety and aggression (Geller, Cooper, Garfinkel, Schwartz-Soicher, & Mincy, 2012).

The preceding discussion demonstrates that many fathers living apart from their children are unable to fulfil their role as provider, but nevertheless seek alternative ways to make meaningful and critical contributions to their development. The frustration of being unable to contribute financially was borne out in the narratives of some of the male offenders interviewed for this study who identified this as the primary motivation for their criminal involvement. An appreciation for the possibility that among these offenders, exist fathers that indeed are 'present' in the lives of their children in a variety of ways, may have important implications for the manner in which they are treated when running afoul of the law.

Discussion

In Chapter 5 I discussed the two opposing schools of thought that are at the centre of the debate as to what should govern judicial sentencing. The first, which limits the autonomy available to judges, operates in the pursuit of consistency, and measures justice by the level of consistency or uniformity that is achieved through sentencing. The consideration of extra-legal factors runs counter to this philosophy since the culpability of the offender must form the basis of the punishment given. In reality, the pursuit of consistency within the context of judicial decision making, though important, may be a futile one since judges routinely disagree on the manner in which the law should be applied, despite being confronted with identical argumentation (Collins, 2005). This is evidenced by the struggle to achieve the desired consistency under the United States Sentencing Reform Act. The second school of thought sees justice as dependent not solely on consistency, but on a consideration of all the factors relevant to a case prior to sentencing. It is based on the belief that no objectively 'right' sentence exists, and that judges must balance innumerable variables in order to come to a holistically appropriate sentence (Mallett, 2015).

While the need for consistency is of fundamental importance to the criminal justice system in any society, as it is essential to maintaining the trust of the public, the deleterious effects of parental incarceration are well documented. To ignore this at the expense of an attempt to achieve uniformity suggests that such effects are deemed unimportant. The Barbados Penal System Reform (Amendment) Act (2014) recognised the need for consistency; however it represented the belief that for justice to be served, there must be a consideration of a range of possible mitigating factors. In keeping with this sentiment, the magistrates interviewed believed that the protection of children warranted special consideration, and the Act gives them the room to apply discretion accordingly. Within a region in which there is considerable concern over rising levels of crime, the need for penal policy that is punitive enough to encourage deterrence is understandable. However, if the welfare of children is indeed the priority, then the evidence presented in this study suggests the need for discretion to be applied to the benefit of all offenders, regardless of sex, who are deemed to be making critical contributions to the development of their children.

This study has revealed an irony in the apparent privileging of the child care responsibilities assumed to be the domain of women, considering that patriarchal relations have presided over the traditional and ongoing undervaluing of domestic work within the region. The patriarchal ideologies upon which the colonial experience was founded trained black men in what Alexander (1994) referred to as 'respectable citizenship' in which they were expected to "render public service to the nation" and adhere to respectable ideals of masculinity, while black women were trained at home and expected to contribute to nation building by producing and caring for the family. The burden of this work is not only feminised, but severely underappreciated (Robinson, 2017). This positioning of women as dependents of men is also reflected in British law where citizenship is perceived as secondary for women. In fact, courts are seen as sites where "gender relations and social hierarchies are dramatized" (Robinson, 2017). Men and women are often impacted negatively by the gender conventions as different rules are created for each which affect them both (Robinson, 2013). This is present not only in the courts but also in state regulations such as the Trinidad and Tobago Police Service Commission Rules which provided that the Commissioner could terminate the appointment of a woman officer who was married on the grounds that her family obligations are affecting the efficient performance of her duties. It is only in 2009 that this law was ruled by the Privy Council as discriminatory (Robinson, 2013).

Further evidence of the undervaluing of child care as well as the subordination of women into this role comes in the form of the dual family justice system which continues to privilege heterosexual unions. In Barbados, long-term heterosexual relationships or marriages can access "contemporary family law rules applied by the more dignified high court, while single women remain restricted to summary courts" (Robinson, 2017, p. 62). The gendered enactment of the law is reflected in the Child Maintenance Act which seeks to hold fathers financially accountable. However, this Act permits men to determine what they can or are willing to contribute financially to their child(ren), ignoring the indirect and direct costs required to care for a child (Robinson, 2017). The Act affirms that child care, including social and financial support, is primarily the responsibility of unmarried mothers.

Ironically however, whereas feminist investigations of gender and the law have suggested that women are often disadvantaged by the legal system (Lazarus-Black, 2001; Soares, 2012), this study demonstrates that these gendered ideologies have been disadvantageous to men when they come into contact with the justice system. In Chapter 5 I noted the manner in which culture affects the law. While legal practitioners are trained to operate outside of the social context, examining each case based on the law, the system also permits discretionary power to judges. Lazarus-Black (2001) posits that where discretionary power is used in interpreting laws, judges "stretch laws in accordance with changing mores and customs". Soares affirms Lazarus-Black's conclusion, noting that "judges in the Caribbean's political and legal systems can be impartial and independent of government and state, once they ruled within the parameters of the law" (Soares, 2012). Beyond this impartiality, it must be acknowledged that judges have been "socialised in a particular political, social and cultural context" which inform their rulings. Women, the 'secondary' citizens who are the mothers and care takers of our nation, may benefit from sentiments that are affected by multiple factors which may, in turn, influence the manner in which they are treated by the court, especially when they have children and/or dependents.

The law is a means of social control, and has been conceptualised to maintain a particular order. The notion of the matrifocal family with a strong black Caribbean woman who sacrifices for her children despite multiple obstacles, and who loves and cares for her family naturally, influences perceptions of women's behaviours and informs the actions of agents of the law. These gendered assumptions permeate our cultural practices and are reproduced within the legal system. At present, assumptions related to the respective domestic roles of men and women mean that men are presumed to play an insignificant role. As such discretion on the part of civil society, police and the judiciary appears to be reserved for women. In this sense, these findings represent a rare occurrence in which patriarchal relations are operating to the detriment of men.

References

Adams, J. (2007). Respect and reputation: The construction of masculinity in poor African American men. *Journal of African American Studies*, 11(3/4), 157–172.

Adler, P. (1994). *Wheeling and Dealing: An Ethnography of an Upper Level Drug Dealing and Smuggling Community*. New York: Columbia University Press.

Agnew, R. (1985). A revised strain theory of delinquency. *Social Forces*, 64, 151–167.

Albonetti, C. (1986). Criminality, prosecutorial screening, and uncertainty: Toward a theory of discretionary decision making in felony case processing. *Criminology*, 24(4), 623–644.

Alcock, P. (1997). *Understanding Poverty*. London: Macmillan.

Alder, C., & Polk, K. (1996). Masculinity and child homicide. *British Journal of Criminolgy*, 36, 396–411.

Alexander, J. (1994). Not just (any) body can be a citizen: The politics of law, sexuality and postcoloniality in Trinidad and Tobago and the Bahamas. *Feminist Review*, 48(1), 5–23.

Allen, H. (1987). *Justice Unbalanced Gender, Psychiatry and Judicial Decisions*. Milton Keynes: Open University Press.

Anderson, E. (1999). *Code of the Street: Decency, Violence, and the Moral Life of the Inner-city*. New York: W. W. Norton and Company Inc.

Anderson, P. (1986). Women in the Caribbean (Part 1). *Social and Economic Studies*, 35, 291–325.

Anderson, P., & Daley, C. (2015). African-Caribbean fathers: The conflict between masculinity and fathering. In J. Roopnarine (Ed.), *Fathers Across Cultures: The Importance, Roles and Diverse Practices of Dads* (pp. 13–38). Santa Barbara, CA: Praeger.

Anthony, T., Bartels, L., & Hopkins, A. (2016). Lessons lost in sentencing: Welding individualised justice to indigenous justice. *University of Technology, Sydney Faculty of Law Legal Studies Research Paper Series*, 2016(1), 47–76.

Antrobus, P. (2004). *The Global Women's Movement: Origins, Issues and Strategies*. Kingston: Ian Randle.

Antrobus, P. (2006). Gender equality in the new millennium: Goal or gimmick? *Caribbean Quarterly*, 52(2/3), 39–50.

Azevedo, M. (2011). The African family and the challenges of the 21st century. In O. Aborampah, & N. Sudaakasa (Eds.), *Extended Families in Africa and the Afrian Diaspora* (pp. 21–44). Trenton, NJ: Africa World Press.

Bailey, C. (2004). *Crime and Social Exclusion in the Kingston Metropolitan Area*. PhD Thesis. Mona: University of the West Indies.

Bailey, C. (2010). Social protection in communities vulnerable to criminal activity. *Social and Economic Studies*, 59(1), 211–242.

Bailey, C. (2016). *Crime and Violence in Barbados: IDB Series on Crime and Violence in the Caribbean*. Washington, DC: Inter-American Development Bank.

Bailey, C., & Coore-Desai, C. (2012). Th effect of exposure to community violence on levels of aggression: Evidence from a sample of Jamaican children. *Childhood*, 19, 188–203.

Bailey, C., Lashley, J., & Barrow, C. (2019). *Rethinking Poverty: Assets, Social Exclusion, Resilience and Human Rights in Barbados*. Jamaica: University of the West Indies Press.

Bailey, W., Branche, C., Jackson, J., & Lee, A. (2004). Fatherhood in risk environments. In B. Bailey, & E. Leo-Rhyne (Eds.), *Gender in the 21st Century: Caribbean Perspectives, Visions and Possibilities* (pp. 162–176). Kingston: Ian Randle.

Bailey, W., Branche, C., & Le Franc, E. (1998). Parenting and socialisation in Caribbean family systems. *Caribbean Dialogue*, 4(1), 21–28.

Bailey, W., Branche, C., McGarritty, S., & Stuart, S. (1998). *Family and the Quality of Gender Relations in the Caribbean*. Jamaica: Institute of Social and Economic Research.

Baird, A. (2012). The violent gang and the construction of masculinity amongst socially excluded young men. *Safer Communities*, 11, 179–190.

Bamfield, J. (2004). Shrinkage, shoplifting and the cost of retail crime in Europe: A cross-sectional analysis of major retailers in 16 European countries. *International Journal of Retail & Distribution Management*, 32(5), 235–241.

Bamfield, J. (2012). *Shopping and Crime*. New York: Palgrave.

Barbados Country Assessment of Living Conditions. (2010). Bridgetown: Sir Arthur Lewis Institute of Social and Economic Studies.

Barbados Penal System Reform (Amendment) Act. (2014, January 9). Barbados Parliament. Retrieved October 2019, from www.barbadosparliament.com/uploads/bill_resolution/afdc3be1356913a10c1f03c48c78711b.pdf

Barbados Statistical Services. (2013). *Population and Housing Census*. Barbados: Barbados Statistical Services.

Barnett, T., & Whiteside, A. (2002). *AIDS in the Twenty-First Century: Disease and Globalisation*. Basingstoke: Palgrave/Macmillan.

Barriteau, E. (2001). *The Political Economy of Gender in the Twentieth Century Caribbean*. Hampshire: Palgrave.

Barriteau, E. (Ed.). (2002). *Gender? What Is It? What Is It Not? A Genealogy of the Concept of Gender and Its Relevance for Policy Makers*. Barbados: University of the West Indies, Centre for Gender and Development Studies, Cave HIll.

Barriteau, E. (2003). Confronting power, theorizing gender in the commonwealth Caribbean. In E. Barriteau (Ed.), *Confronting Power, Theorizing Gender: Interdisciplinary Perspectives in the Caribbean* (pp. 3–24). Kingston: University of the West Indies Press.

Barros, G. (2010). Herbert A. Simon and the concept of rationality: Boundaries and procedures. *Brazilian Journal of Political Economy*, 30(3), 455–472.

Barros, R., Ferreira, F, Molinas, J., & Chanduvi, J. (2009). *Measuring Inequality of Opportunities in Latin America and the Caribbean*. Washington, DC: World Bank.

Barrow, C. (1986). Anthropology, the family and women in the Caribbean. *Concerning Women and Development*, 86, 1–9.

Barrow, C. (1996). *Family in the Caribbean: Themes and Perspectives*. Kingston: Ian Randle.

Barrow, C. (2001). Men, women and family in the Caribean: A review. In C. Barrow, & R. Reddock (Eds.), *Caribbean Sociology: Introductory Readings* (pp. 418–426). Jamaica: Ian Randle.

Barrow, C., & Reddock, R. (2001). *Caribbean Sociology: Introductory Readings*. Jamaica: Ian Randle.

BBC. (2003, September 13). Jamaica's Women Drug Mules Fill UK Jails. Retrieved October 22, 2019, from news.bbc.co.uk/2/hi/3097882.stm

Beckles, H., & Shepherd, V. (2000). *Caribbean Slavery in the Atlantic World: A Student Reader*. Kingston: Ian Randle.

Beneria, L., & Sen, G. (1981). Accumulation, reproduction, and women's role in economic development: Boserup revisited. *Signs: Developement and the Sexual Division of Labour*, 7(2), 279–298.

Bickle, G., & Peterson, R. (1991). The impact of gender based family roles on criminal sentencing. *Social Problems*, 38, 372–394.

Biddle, B. (1979). *Role Theory: Expectations, Identities and Behaviours*. London: Academic Press.

Biddle, B. (1986). Recent developments in role theory. *Annual Review of Sociology*, 12, 67–92.

Bissessar, A. (2013). The nexus between structural adjustment and emergence of gangs: The case of Trinidad and Tobago. In R. Seepersad, & A. Bissessar (Eds.), *Gangs in the Caribbean* (pp. 131–149). Newcastle: Cambridge Scholars Publishing.

Blanco, C., Grant, J., Petry, N., Simpson, H., Alegria, A., Liu, S., & Hasin, D. (2008). Prevalence and correlates of shoplifting in the United States: Results from the National Epidemiologic Survey on alcohol and related conditions (NESARC). *American Journal of Psychiatry*, 165(7), 905–913.

Blank, S. (2013). An historical and contemporary overview of gendered Caribbean relations. *Journal of Arts and Humanities*, 2(4), 1–10.

Blossfeld, H., & Hofmeister, H. (2006). *Globalization, Uncertainty and Women's Careers: An International Comparison*. Cheltenham: Edwards Elgar Publishing.

Bocock, R. (1993). *Cosumption*. London: Routledge.

Bourne, C. (2005). Poverty and Its Alleviation in the Caribbean. Lecture presented at the Alfred O. Heath Distinguished Speakers Forum. University of the Virgin Islands. The Virgin Islands.

Boxill, I., & Quarless, R. (2005). The determinants of poverty among the youth of the Caribbean. *Social and Economic Studies*, 54(1), 129–160.

Brashear-Tiede, L. (2009). The impact of the federal sentencing guidelines and reform: A comparative analysis. *Justice System Journal*, 30, 34–49.

Brereton, B. (1998). Gendered testimonies: Autobiographies, diaries and letters by women as sources for Caribbean history. *Feminist Review*, 59(1), 143–163.

Britton, D. (2003). *At Work in the Iron Cage: The Prison as Gendered Organization*. New York: University Press.

Britton, D. (2011). *The Gender of Crime*. Lanham, MD: Rowman and Littlefield.

Brown, I., & Misra, J. (2003). The intersection of race and gender in the labour market. *Annual Review of Sociology*, 29, 487–513.

Brown, J. (1995). *Gender Relations and Conflict in Fathering*. Washington, DC: World Bank.

Brown, J., Anderson, P., & Chevannes, B. (1993). *The Contribution of Caribbean Men to the Family*. Kingston: Caribbean Child Development Centre.

Brown, M. (1981). *Working in the Street: Police Discretion and the Dilemmas of Reform*. New York: Sage Foundation.

Burchell, B. (1994). The effects of labour market postion on job insecurity and unemployment on psychological health. In D. Gallie, C. Marsh, & C. Vogler (Eds.), *Social Change and the Experience of Unemployment* (pp. 118–212). Oxford: Oxford University Press.

Bush, B. (1990). *Slave Women in Caribbean Society 1650–1838*. Kingston: Heinemann Publishers.

Cameron, M. (1964). *The Booster and the Snitch*. New York: Free Press.

Caputo, G., & King, A. (2011). Shoplifting: Work, agency, and gender. *Feminist. Criminology*, 6(3), 159–177.

Carby, H. (1997). White women listen! Black feminism and the boundaries of sisterhood. In H. Mirza (Ed.), *Black British Feminism: A Reader* (pp. 45–53). New York: Routledge.

CARICOM. (2003). *Women and Men in the Caribbean Community: Facts and Figures*. Guyana: CARICOM.

Carlen, P. (1992). Criminal women and criminal justice, the limits to, and the potential of, feminist and left realist perspectives. In R. Mathews, & J. Young (Eds.), *Issues in Realist Criminology* (pp. 475–483). London: Sage.

Chamberlain, M. (2010). *Empire and Nation-Builliding in the Caribbean: Barbados, 1937–1966*. Manchester: Manchester University Press.

Cheadle, J., Amato, P., & King, V. (2010). Patterns of nonresident father contact. *Demography*, 47, 205–225.

Chesney-Lind, M., & Rodriguez, N. (1983). Women under lock and key: A view from the inside. *The Prison Journal*, 63, 47–65.

Chesney-Lind, M., & Shelden, R. (1992). *Girls, Delinquency, and Juvenile Justice*. Belmont, CA: Wadsworth.

Chevannes, B. (2001). *Learning to be a Man: Culture, Socialisation and Gender*. Jamaica: University of the West Indies Press.

Clarke, E. (1966). *My Mother Who Fathered Me*. London: George Allen & Unwin Ltd.

Clarke, M., & Henry-Lee, A. (2005). *Women in Prison: The Impact of the Incarceration of Jamaican Women on Themsleves and Their Families*. Jamaica: Planning Institute of Jamaica.

Cohen, A. (1955). *Delinquent Boys*. Chicago, IL: Glencoe Free Press.

Coleman, J., & Hong, Y. (2008). Beyond nature and nurture: The influence of lay gendr theories on self stereotyping. *Self and Identity*, 7, 34–53.

Coles, R., & Green, C. (2010). *The Myth of the Missing Black Father*. New York: Columbia University.

Collins, P. (2000). *Black Feminist Thought Knowledge, Consciousness, and the Politics of Empowerment*. New York: Unwin Hyman.

Collins, P. (2005). The consistency of judicial choice. Paper Prepared For Delivery at the 101st Annual Meeting of the American Political Science Association. Washington, DC.

Collins, W., Maccoby, E., Steinberg, L., Hetherington, E., & Bornstein, M. (2000). Contemporary research on parenting: The case for nature and nurture. *American Psychologist*, 55(2), 218–232.

Condry, J., & Condry, S. (1976). Sex differences: A study in the eye of the beholder. *Child Development*, 47, 812–819.

Connell, R. (1995). *Masculinities*. Berkley: University of California Press.

Connell, R., & Messerschmidt, J. (2005). Hegemonic masculinity: Rethinking the concept. *Gender and Society*, 19(6), 829–859.

Contreras, R. (2009). Damn yo – who's that girl? An ethnographic analysis of masculinity in drug robberies. *Journal of Contemporary Ethnography*, 38(4), 465–492.

Cornia, G. (2010). Income distribution under Latin America's new left regimes. *Journal of Human Development and Capabilities*, 11(1), 85–114.

Covington, J. (1985). Gender differences in criminality among heroin users. *Journal of Research in Crime and Delinquency*, 22(4), 329–353.

Crenshaw, K. (1989). Demarginalizing the intersection of race and sex: A black feminist critique of antidiscrimination doctrine, feminist theory and antiracist politics. *University of Chicago Legal Forum*, 1989(8), 139.

Crenshaw, K. (1991). Mapping the margins: Intersectionality, identity politics and violence against women of colour. *Stanford Law Review*, 43(6), 1241–1299.

Cullen, A., & Hodgetts, D. (2001). Unemployment as illness: An exploration of accounts voiced by unemployment in Aotearoa/New Zealand. *Analyses of Social Issues and Public Policy*, 1(1), 33–51.

Curry, T., Lee, G., & Rodriguez, S. (2004). Does victim gender increase sentence severity? Further explorations of gender dynamics and sentencing outcomes. *Crime and Delinquency*, 50, 319–343.

Dabney, D., Hollinger, C., & Dugan, L. (2004). Who actually steals? A study of covertly observed shoplifters. *Justice Quarterly*, 21(4), 693–672.

Daly, K. (1987). Structure and practice of familial-based justice in a criminal court. *Law and Society Review*, 21(2), 267–290.

Daly, K., & Bort, R. (1995). Sex effect and sentencing: A review of the statistical literature. *Justice Quarterly*, 12(1), 143–177.

Dann, K. (1987). *The Barbadian Male: Sexual Attitudes and Practice*. London: McMillan.

Dasgupta, N. (2013). Implicit attitudes and beliefs adapt to situations: A decade of research on the malleability of implicit prejudice, stereotypes and the self-concept. *Advances in Experimental Social Psychology*, 47, 233–279.

Datcher, M. (2001). *Raising Fences: A Black Man's Love Story*. New York: Riverhead Books.

Davidson, L. (2015, July 23). Shoplifting in Russia is soaring as the economy crumbles. Retrieved September 2019, from *The Telegraph*: www.telegraph.co.uk/finance/economics/11759336/Shoplifting-in-Russia-is-soaring-as-the-economy-crumbles.html

Davies, P. (1999). *Women, crime and an infromal economy*. Paper presented to the British Criminology Conference, July 1997. Queens University Belfast, Belfast.

DeKeseredy, W., & Schwartz, M. (2005). Masculinities and interpersonal violence. In M. Kimmel, J. Hearn, & R. Connell (Eds.), *Handbook of Studies on Men and Masculinities* (pp. 353–366). Thousand Oaks, CA: Sage.

Demuth, S., & Steffensmeier, D. (2004). The impact of gender and race-ethnicity in the pretrial release process. *Social Problems*, 51(2), 222–242.

Desai, N., & Krishnaraj, M. (2004). An overview of the status of women in India. In M. Manoranjan (Ed.), *Class, Caste, Gender* (pp. 296–319). New Delhi: Sage Publications.

Dickenson, D. (2000). Crime and unemployment: Despite Tory denials there is a clear link between them. *New Economy*, 2(2), 115–120.

Dixon, J. (1995). The organizational context of criminal sentencing. *American Journal of Sociology*, 100, 1157–1198.

Downes, A. (2010). *Poverty and Its Reduction in the Small Developing Countries of the Caribbean. Ten Years of 'War Against Poverty'*. Manchester: Chronic Poverty Research Centre, University of Manchester.

Eagly, A., & Wood, W. (2011). Social role theory. In P. Van Lange, A. Kruglanski, & E. Higgins (Eds.), *Handbook of Theories in Social Psychology* (pp. 458–476). Thousand Oaks, CA: Sage Publications.

Eagly, A., Wood, W., & Diekman, A. (2000). Social role theory of sex differences and similarities: A current appraisal. In T. Eckles, & H. Trautner (Eds.), *The Developmental Social Psychology of Gender* (pp. 123–174). Mahwah, NJ: Lawrence Erlbaum Associates Publishers.

Editorial. (2002, August 13). Ja, the UK and the drug trade. *Jamaica Observer*.

Epp, C., Maynard-Moody, S., & Haider-Markel, D. (2016). Beyond profiling: The institutional sources of racial disparities in policing. *Public Administration Review*, 77(2), 168–178.

Esmee Fairbairn Foundation. (2003). *A Bitter Pill to Swallow: The Sentencing of Foreign National Drug Couriers*. London: Esmee Fairbairn Foundation.

Evans, H., & Davies, R. (1997). Overview of issues in childhood socialization in the Caribbean. In J. Roopnarine, & J. Brown (Eds.), *Caribbean Families: Diversity Among Ethnic Groups*. London: Ablex.

Evans, R., Gauthier, D., & Forsyth, C. (1998). Dogfighting: Symbolic expression and validation of manhood. *Sex Roles*, 39(11/12), 825–838.

Farmer, J., & Dawson, J. (2017). American college students' shoplifting expereince: A comparison of retrospective self-reports to micro-level criminological theory. *International Journal of criminal Justice Sciences*, 12(1), 1–23.

Federal Bureau of Investigation. (2014). Uniform Crime Reports. Retrieved March 2019, from https://ucr.fbi.gov/crime-in-the-u.s

Flanagan, T., & Maguire, K. (Eds.). (1990). *Sourcebook of Criminal Justice Statistics 1989*. Washington, DC: US Government Printing Office.

Fleetwood, J. (2015). A narrative approach to women's law breaking. *Feminist Criminology*, 10(4), 368–388.

Ford, R. (2003, August 6). Prison crisis as foreign inmates soar: Overcrowding fuelled by drug smuggling convictions. Retrieved from *The Times*: www.thetimes.co.uk/tto/news/uk/article1956532.ece

Francis, A., Gibbison, G., Harriott, A., & Kirton, C. (2009). *Crime and Development: The Jamaican Experience*. Kingston: Sir Arthur Lewis Institute of Social and Economic Studies, University of the West Indies.

Francis, D. (1979). *Shoplifting: The Crime Everybody Pays For*. New York: Elsevier Nelson Books.

Frederick, C. (2010). *The Caribbean is the Fragile Third Border of Drug Trafficking*. Washington, DC: Council on Hemispheric Affairs.

Freiburger, T. (2010). The effects of gender, family status, and race on sentencing decisions. *Behaviour Sciences and Law*, 28, 378–395.

Freiburger, T. (2011). The impact of gender, offense type, and familial role on the decision to incarcerate. *Social Justice Research*, 24, 143–167.

Freud, S. (1933). *New Introductory Lectures on Psychoanalysis*. New York: W. W. Norton.

Fryer, R. (2016). *An empirical analysis of racial differences in police use of force* (No. w22399). National Bureau of Economic Research.

Gaines, K., & Glensor, R. (2004). *Policing in America* (Vol. 4). Cincinnati, OH: Anderson Publishing.

Gallie, D., & Vogler, C. (1994). Unmployment and attitudes to work. In D. Gallie, C. Marsh, & V. C (Eds.), *Social Change and the Experience of Unemployment* (pp. 1–30). Oxford: Oxford University Press.

Geiger, B. (2006). Crime, prostitution, drugs, and insanity: Female offenders' resistant strategies to abuse and domination. *International Journal of Offender Therapy and Comparative Criminology*, 50, 582–594.

Geller, A., Cooper, C., Garfinkel, I., Schwartz-Soicher, O., & Mincy, R. (2012). Beyond absenteeism: Father incarceration and child development. *Demography*, 49(1), 49–76.

Giddens, A. (1993). *Sociology*. Cambridge: Polity Press.

Gilmore, D. (1990). *Manhood in the Making: Cultural Concepts of Masculinity*. New Haven, CT: Yale University Press.

Giroux, H. (2008). *Against the Terror of Neoliberalism: Politics Beyond the Age of Greed*. Boulder, CO: Paradigm Publishers.

Glaze, L., & Maruschack, L. (2008). Parents in prison and their minor children. Bureau of Justice Statistics: Special Report.

Goel, S., Rao, J., & Shroff, R. (2016). Precinct or prejudice? Understanding racial disparities in New York City's stop-and-frisk policy. *The Annals of Applied Statistics*, 10(1), 365–394.

Goffman, E. (1959). *The Presentation of Self in Everyday Life*. New York: Anchor Books.

Government of Jamaica. (2002). *Report on the National Committee on Crime and Violence*. Jamaica: Government of Jamaica.

Green, A. (2017). *A Generative Perspective of Afro-Jamaican Fathers' Socialization of Values for their Children in Middle Childhood*. MSc Thesis. Ontario: University of Guelph.

Grewal, I., & Kaplan, C. (1994). Introduction: Transnational practices and questions of postmodernity. In I. Grewal, & C. Kaplan (Eds.), *Scattered Hegemonies: Postmodernity and transnational Feminist Practices* (pp. 1–33). Minneapolis: University of Minnesotta Press.

Hairston, C. (1998). The forgottenparent: Understanding the forces that influence incarcerated fathers' relationships with their children. *Child Welfare: Journal of Policy, Practice, and Program*, 77(5), 617–637.

Hall, S. (2002). Reflections on race, articulation and societies structured in dominance. In P. Essed, & T. Goldgerg (Eds.), *Race Critical Theories* (pp. 449–454). Malden, MA: Blackwell.

Halsey, A., Heath, A., & Ridge, J. (1980). *Origins and Destinations*. Oxford: Clarendon Press.

Hamer, J. (2001). *What it Means to be a Daddy: Fatherhood for Black Men Living Away From Their Children*. New York: Columbia University Press.

Hamilton, M. (2017). Sentencing disparities. *British Journal of American Legal Studies*, 176, 177–224.

Handwerker, W. (1991). Women's power and fertility transition: The cases of Africa and the West Indies. *Population and Environment*, 13(1), 55–78.

Handwerker, W. (1992). West Indian gender relations, family planning programs and fertility decline. *Social Science and Medicine*, 15(10), 1245–1257.

Harriott, A. (2000). *Police and Crime Control in Jamaica*. Kingston: University of the West Indies Press.

Harriott, A. (2003). The Jamaican crime problem: New developments and new challenges for public policy. In A. Harriott (Ed.), *Understanding Crime in Jamaica: New Challenges for Public Policy* (pp. 63–88). Jamaica: Universtiy of the West Indies Press.

Harris, A. (2008). The social construction of "sophisticated" adolescents: How judges integrate juvenile and criminal justice decision-making models. *Journal of Contemporary Ethnography*, 37, 469–506.

Hartley, R., Maddan, S., & Spohn, C. (2007). Concerning conceptualization and operationalization: Sentencing data and the focal concerns perspective – A research note. *The Southwest Journal of Criminal Justice*, 4, 58–78.

Hawkins, D. (1981). Causal attribution and punishment for crime. *Deviant Behaviour*, 2(3), 207–230.

Hay, C. (2003). Family strain, gender and delinquency. *Sociological Perspectives*, 46(1), 107–135.

Hearn, J., & Collinson, D. (2006). Men, masculinities and workplace diversity. In A. Konrad, P. Pushkala, & J. Pringle (Eds.), *Handbook of Workplace Diversity* (pp. 299–322). London: Sage.

Heidensohn, F. (1994). Gender and crime. In M. Maguire, R. Morgan, & R. Reiner (Eds.), *The Oxford Handbook of Criminology* (pp. 997–1039). Oxford: Clarendon Press.

Henry-Lee, A. (2002). Economic deprivation and private adjustments: The case of security guards in Jamaica. *Social and Economic Studies*, 51(4), 181–209.

Herbert, S. (1955). A behavioural model of rational choice. *The Quarterly Journal of Economics*, 69(1), 99–118.

Hill, B. (1999). *The Strengths of African American Families: Twenty-Five Years Later.* Lanham, MD: University Press of America.

Hindelang, M. (1974). Decisions of shoplifting victims to invoke the criminal justice process. *Social Problems*, 21, 580–593.

Hirtenlehner, H., Blackwell, B., Leitgoeb, H., & Bacher, J. (2014). Explaining the gender gap in juvenile shoplifting: A power-control theoretical analysis. *Deviant Behaviour*, 35(1), 41–65.

Hochstetler, A., & Copes, H. (2003). Situational construction of masculinity among male street thieves. *Journal of Contemporary Ethnography*, 32, 279–304.

Hofer, P., Blackwell, K., & Ruback, R. (1999). The effect of federal sentencing guidelines on inter-judge sentencing disparities. *The Journal of Criminal Law and Criminology*, 90, 239–306.

Hollinger, R., & Davis, J. (2002). *2002 National Retail Security Survey.* Gainesville: University of Florida.

Hooks, B. (2004). *The Will to Change: Men, Masculinity and Love.* New York: Atria Books.

Horace, W., & Rohlin, S. (2016). How dark is light? Bright lights, big city, racial profiling. *The Review of Economics and Statistics*, 98(2), 226–232.

Horowitz, R., & Pottieger, A. (1991). Gender bias in juvenile justice handling of seriously crime-involved youth. *Journal of Research in Crime and Delinquency*, 28, 75–100.

Huebner, B., & Gustafson, R. (2007). The effect of maternal incarceration on adult offspring invovlement in the criminal justice system. *Journal of Criminal Justice*, 35, 283–296.

Hughes, E. (1945). Dilemmas and contradictions of status. *American Journal of Sociology*, 353–359.

Jamaica Observer. (2011, August 4). Barbados Police Nab 8 Jamaican Drug mules. Retrieved October 22, 2011, from jamaicaobserver.com/news/police-nab-8-Jamaican-drug-mules

James, L. (2018). The stability of implicit racial bias in police officers. *Police Quarterly*, 21(1), 30–52.

Kambon, A., & Henderson, G. (2008). *Exploring Policy Linkahes Between Poverty, Crime, and Violence: A Look at Three Caribbean States.* Port of Spain: ECLAC.

Katz, J. (1988). *The Seductions of Crime.* New York: Basic Books.

Katz, R. (2000). Explaining girls' and women's crime and desistance in the context of their victimization experiences. *Violence Against Women*, 6, 633–660.

Kellor, F. (1901). *Experimental Sociology: Descriptive and Analytical.* New York: The Macmillan Company.

Kelly, L., Lovett, J., & Regan, L. (2005). *A Gap or Chasm? Attrition in Reported Rape Cases.* London: HMSO.

Kerr, J. (1997). *Report of the National Committe on Political Tribalism.* Kingston: Jamaica Information Service.

Klein, D., & Kreis, J. (1976). Any woman's blues: A critical overview of women, crime and the criminal justice system. *Crime and Social Justice*, 5, 34–49.

Kloppenburg, S. (2013). Mapping the contours of mobility regimes. Air travel and drug smuggling between the Caribbean and the Netherlands. *Mobilities*, 8(1), 52–69.

Kramer, J., & Ulmer, J. (2006). Downward departures for serious violent offenders: Local court "corrections" to Pennsylvania's sentencing guidelines. *Criminology*, 40(4), 897–932.

Krasnovsky, T., & Lane, R. (1998). Shoplifting: A review of the literature. *Aggression and Violent Behavior*, 3, 219–236.

Kray, L., Howland, L., Russell, A., & Jackman, L. (2016). The effects of implicit gender role theories on gender system justification: Fixed beliefs strengthen masculinity to preserve the status quo. *Journal of Personality and Social Psychology*, 11, 98–115.

Krohn, M., Curry, J., & Nelson-Kilger, S. (1983). Is chivalry dead? An analysis of changes in police dispositions of males and females. *Criminology: An Interdisciplinry Journal*, 21(3), 417–437.

Kruttschnitt, C. (1982). Women, crime, and delinquency: An application of the theory of law. *Criminology*, 19, 495–513.

Lazarus-Black, M. (2001). My mother never fathered me: Rethinking kinship and the governing of families. In C. Barrow, & R. Reddock (Eds.), *Caribbean Sociology: Introductory Readings* (pp. 389–402). Kingston: Ian Randle.

Lee, H., McCormick, T., Hicken, M., & Wildeman, C. (2015). Racial inequalities in connectedness to imprisoned individuals in the United States. *DuBois Review*, 12(1), 1–14.

Leighton, K. (2012). *The Scandal of Inequality in Latin American and the Caribbean.* London: Christian Aid.

Leo-Rhynie, E. (2002). Women in development studies. In P. Mohammed (Ed.), *Gendered Realities: Essays in Caribbean Feminist Thought* (pp. 147–163). Mona: University of the West Indies Press.

Lerner, G. (1986). *The Creation of Patriarchy.* Oxford: Oxford University Press.

Letkemann, P. (1973). *Crime as Work.* Englewood Cliffs, NJ: Prentice Hall.

Levy, H. (1996). *They Cry Respect: Urban Violence and Poverty in Jamaica.* Mona: Department of Sociology, University of the West Indies.

Lewis, L. (2004a). Caribbean masculinity at the Fin de Siecle. In R. Reddock (Ed.), *Interrogating Caribbean Masculinities* (pp. 244–266). Kingston: UWI Press.

Lewis, L. (2004b). Masculinity, the political economy of the body and patriarchal power in the Caribbean. In B. Bailey, & E. Leo-Rhynie (Eds.), *Gender in the 21st Century: Caribbean Perspectives Visions and Possibilities* (pp. 236–261). Kingston: Ian Randle.

Lewis, O. (1965). *La Vida.* New York: Random House.

Lin, J., Grattet, R., & Petersilia, J. (2010). 'Back end sentencing' and reimprisonment: Individual, organizational and community predictors of parole sentencin decisions. *Criminology,* 48(3), 759–795.

Loeber, R., Farrington, D., Stouthamer-Loeber, M., & Van Kammen, W. (1998). *Antisocial Behaviour and Mental Health Problems: Explanatory Factors in Childhood and Adolescence.* Mahwah, NJ: Lawrence Earlbaum.

Lombroso, C., & Ferrero, W. (1958). *The Female Offender, Reprint.* New York: New York Philosophical Library.

Lorde, A. (1984). *Sister Outsider.* Freedom, CA: Crossing Press.

Lynch, M., Omori, M., Roussell, A., & Valasik, M. (2013). Policing the progressive city: The racialized geography of drug law enforcement. *Theoretical Criminology,* 17(2), 335–357.

Macrae, C., Stangor, C., & Hewstone, M. (1996). *Stereotypes and Stereotyping.* New York: The Guilford Press.

Maher, L. (1997). *Sexed Owrk: Gender, Race and Resistance in a Brooklyn Drug Market.* New York: Oxford University Press.

Mair, L. (2006). *A Historical Study of Women in Jamaica.* Kingston: University of the West Indies Press.

Mallett, S. (2015). Judicial discretion in sentencing: A justice system that is no longer just? Retrieved March 2019, from Paper Submitted in Fulfillment of LLB Degree: https://pdfs.semanticscholar.org/cc56/788b05de1b85f2f-caa85d281ab91ce5f1db5.pdf

Manninen, S. (2013). Masculinity and respect in flux: Olli's story. *Gender and Education,* 25(7), 872–888.

Markrian v The Queen, 25 (High Court of Australia 2005).

Merton, R. (1949). *Social Theory and Social Structure: Toward the Codification of Theory and Research.* Glencoe, IL: Free Press.

Messerschmidt, J. (1993). *Masculinities and Crime: Critique and Reconceptualization of Theory.* Lanham, MD: Rowan and Little Field.

Messerschmidt, J. (2000). Becoming 'real men'. *Men and Masculinities,* 2(3), 286–307.

Mezey, N. (2001). Law as culture. *Yale Journal of Law and the Humanities,* 13(1), 35–67.

Miller, E. (1978). *Odd Jobs: The World of Deviant Work.* Englewood Cliffs, NJ: Prentice Hall.

Miller, J. (2002). The strengths and limits of "doing gender" for understadning street crime. *Theoretical Criminology,* 6(4), 433–460.

Millet, K. (1969). *Sexual Politics.* London: Virago.

Mishra, S., Behera, D., & Babu, B. (2012). Socialisation and gender bias at the household level among school-attending girls in a tribal community of the Kalahandi district of Eastern India. *Anthropological Notebooks*, 18(2), 45–53.

Moghadam, V. (2005). *Globalizing Women: Transnational Feminist Networks.* Baltimore, MD: The John Hopkins Universtiy Press.

Mohammed, P. (1995). Writing gender into history: The negotiation of gender relations among indian men and women in post- indenture Trinidad and Tobago, 1917–1947. In V. Shepherd, B. Brereton, P. Mohammed, & A. Perkins (Eds.), *Engendering History: Caribbean Women in Historical Perspective*. Kingston: Ian Randle.

Mohammed, P. (2003). Like sugar in coffee: Third wave feminism and the Caribbean. *Social and Economic Studies*, 52(3), 5–30.

Mohammed, P., & Perkins, A. (1999). *Caribbean Women at the Crossroads: The Paradox of Motherhood among Women of Barbados, St. Lucia and Dominica*. Kingston: Canoe Press. UWI.

Mohanty, C., & Alexander, J. (1997). *Feminist Genealogies, Colonial Legacies, Democratic Futures*. New York: Routledge.

Molinas, J., Barros, R., Saavedra, J., Giugale, M., Cord, L., Pessino, C., & Hasan, A. (2010). *Do Our Children Have a Chance? The 2010 Human Opportunity Report for Latin America and the Caribbean*. Washington, DC: World Bank.

Momsen, J. (1993). *Women and Change in the Caribbean: A Pan-Caribbean Perspective*. Indiana: Indiana University Press.

Moore, R. (1983). Shoplifting in middle America: Patterns and motivational correlates. *Journal of Offender Therapy and Comparative Criminology*, 28, 53–64.

Morris, A. (1987). *Women, Crime and Criminal Justice*. Oxford: Basil Blackwell.

Morris, J., Cook, D., & Shaper, A. (1994). Loss of employment and mortality. *Brititsh Medical Journal*, 308, 1135–1139.

Morrison, W. (1902). The professional criminal in England. *International Journal of Ethics*, 13(1), 27–40.

Moschis, G. (1987). *Consumer Socialization: A Life-Cycle Perspective*. Lexington, KY: Lexington Books.

Moser, C., & Holland, J. (1997). *Urban Poverty and Violence in Jamaica*. Washington, DC: World Bank.

Motley, R., & Joe, S. (2018). Police use of force by ethnicity, sex, and socioeconomic class. *Journal of the Society for Social Work and Research*, 9(1), 49–67.

Moulds, E. (1978). Chivalry and paternalism: Disparities of treatment in the criminal justice system. *Western Political Quarterly*, 31, 416–430.

Mullins, C. (2006). *Holding Your Square: Masculinities, Streetlife and Violence*. Cullompton: Willan.

Murray, J., Loeber, R., & Pardini, D. (2012). Parental criminal justice involvement and the development of youth theft, drug use, depression and educational performance. *Criminology*, 50, 255–302.

Murray, J., & Murray, L. (2010). Parental incarceration, attachement and child psychopathology. *Attachment and Human Development*, 12, 289–309.

Murray, R. (2015). *Too much presence? Men's interests and male intersectionality*. Paper prepared for presentation at the European Conference on Politics and Gender. Uppsala.

Nagel, I., & Hagan, J. (1983). Gender and crime: Offense patterns and criminal court sanctions. Articles by Maurer Faculty 2072. *Crime and Justice*, 4, 91–144.

Nagel, S., & Weitzman, L. (1971). Woman as litigants. *Hastings Law Journal*, 23, 171–198.

NCVS. (2012). *National Crime Victimization Survey: Victimizations Not Reported to the Police, 2006–2010*. Washington, DC: US Department of Justice, Bureau of Justice Statistics.

Nix, J., Campbell, B., Byers, E., & Alpert, G. (2017). A bird's eye view of civilians killed by police in 2015: Further evidence of shooter bias. *Criminology*, 16, 253–276.

Nuttal, C., Eversley, D., Rudder, I., & Ramsay, J. (2003). *The Barbados Crime Survey: Views and Beliefs about Crime and Criminal Justice*. Bridgetown: Department of the Attorney General.

Oliver, M. (1994). *The Violent Social World of the Black Male*. New York: Lexington Books.

Park, R., Burgess, E., & McKensie, R. (1928). *The City*. Chicago, IL: University of Chicago Press.

Parker, K., & Maggard, S. (2005). Structural theories and race-specific drug arrests: What structural factors account for the rise in race-specific drug arrests over time? *Crime and Delinquency*, 51(4), 521–547.

Parsons, T., & Bales, R. (Eds.). (1955). *Family, Socialization and Interaction Process*. New York: Free Press.

Parsons, T., & Bales, R. (1956). *Family, Socialization, and Interaction Process*. London: Routledge and Kegan Paul.

Pettiway, L. (1987). Arson for revenge: The role of environmental situation, age, sex and race. *Journal of Quantitative Criminology*, 3(2), 169–184.

Phillips, S., & Harm, N. (1998). Women prisoners: A contextual framework. In J. Harden, & M. Hill (Eds.), *Breaking the Rules: Women in Prison and Feminist Therapy* (pp. 1–9). New York: Harrington Park Press.

Pitt-Rivers, J. (1968). Honor. In D. Sills (Ed.), *International Encyclopedia of the Social Sciences* (Vol. 6, pp. 506–510). New York: Macmillan Company.

Pitts, L. (1999). Low-Income fathers. *Annual Review of Sociology*, 30, 427–451.

Plant, E., & Peruche, B. (2005). The consequences of race for police officers' responses to criminal suspects. *Psychological Science*, 16(3), 180–183.

Pleck, J., & Masciadrelli, B. (2004). Paternal involvement by US residential fathers: Levels, sources and consequences. In M. E. Lamb (Ed.), *The Role of the Father in Child Development* (pp. 222–271). Hoboken, NJ: John Wiley and Sons.

Pollack, O. (1950). *The Criminality of Women*. Philadelphia: University of Philadelphia Press.

Potter, R. B., Barker, D., Conway, D., & Klak, T. (2014). *The Contemporary Caribbean*. London: Routeledge Taylor & Francis Group.

Puryear, J., & Malloy-Jewers, M. (2009). *How Poor and Unequal is Latin American and the Caribbean?* Washington, DC: Inter-American Dialogue.

Puzzanchera, C. (2000). *Self-Reported Delinquency by 12 year Olds*. Washington, DC: Department of Justice, Office of Juvenile Justice and Delinquency Prevention.

Quinlan, R., & Flinn, M. (2005). Kinship, sex, and fitness in the Caribbean community. *Human Nature*, 16(1), 32–57.

Radosh, P. (2002). Reflections on women's crime and mothers in prison: A peacemaking approach. *Crime and Delinquency*, 48, 300–315.

Raeder, M. (1993). Gender and sentencing: Single moms, battered women, and other sex-bases anomolies in the gendr-free world of the federal sentencing guidelines. *Pepperdine Law Review*, 20(3), 905–990.

Ramsay, K. (2013). *Homicides in Barbados 1980–2010*. Bridgetown: National Task Force on Crime Prevention.

Reddock, R. (1998). Feminism and feminist thought: Consensu and controversy. In P. Mohammed, & C. Shepherd (Eds.), *Gender in Caribbean Development* (pp. 53–73). Jamaica, Trinidad and Tobago, Barbados: University of the West Indies. Women and Development Studies Project.

Reddock, R., & Bobb-Smith, Y. (2008). *Reconciling work and family: Issues and policies in Trinidad and Tobago*. Conditions of Work and Employment Series No. 18. Geneva: ILO.

Reynolds, T. (2009). Exploring the absent/present dilemma: Black fathers, family relationships, and social capital in Britain. *The Annals of the American Academy of Political and Social Science*, 624, 12–28.

Ricciardelli, R. (2011). Masculinity, consumerism, and appearance: A look at men's hair. *Canadian Review of Sociology*, 48(2), 181–201.

Ricketts, H., & Anderson, P. (2008). THe impact of poverty and stress on the interaction of Jamaican caregivers with young children. *International Journal of Early Years Education*, 16, 61–74.

Ridgeway, G. (2006). Assessing the effect of race bias in post-traffic stop outcomes using propensity scores. *Journal of Quantitative Criminology*, 22(1), 1–29.

Ritchie, B. (1996). *Compelled to Crime: The Gender Entrapment of Battered Black Women*. New York: Routledge.

Robinson, T. (2003). Beyond the bill of rights: Sexing the citizen. In Barriteau (Ed.), *Confronting Power, Theorizing Gender: Interdisciplinary Perspectives in the Caribbean* (pp. 231–261). Jamaica: UWI Press.

Robinson, T. (2013). Gender, equality, justice and Caribbean realities: The way forward. Equality, Justice and Caribbean Realities – The Way Forward. Caribbean Association of Judicial Officers (CAJO) 3rd Biennial Conference, Barbados.

Robinson, T. (2017). Valuing caring work. *Journal of Eastern Caribbean Studies*, 42(3), 59–79.

Rodriguez, S., Curry, T., & Lee, G. (2006). Gender differences in criminal sentencing: Do effects vary across violent, property, and drug offenses? *Social Science Quarterly*, 87, 318–339.

Rogers, P., & Davies, M. (2007). Perceptions of victims and perpetrators in a depicted child sexual abuse case: Gender and age factors. *Journal of Interpersonal Violence*, 22(5), 566–584.

Rosaldo, M., & Lamphere, L. (Eds.). (1974). *Women, Culture and Society*. Stanford, CA: Stanford University Press.

Rosen, L. (2006). *Law as Culture: An Invitation*. Princeton, NJ: Princeton University Press.

Rowley, M. (2002). Reconceptualising voice: The role of matrifocality in shaping theories and Caribbean voices. In P. Mohammed (Ed.), *Gendered Realities: Essays in Caribbean Feminist Thought* (pp. 22–43). Barbados: UWI Press.

Rowley, M. (2003). Crafting maternal citizens? Public discourses of the 'maternal scourge' in social welfare policies and services in Trinidad. *Social and Economic Studies (Focus on Gender)*, 52(3), 31–58.

Safa, H. (1995). *The Myth of the Male Breadwinner: Women and Industrialization in the Caribbean*. Oxford: Westview Press.

Schafer, J., & Mastrofski, S. (2005). Police leniency in traffic enforcement encounters: Exploratory findings from observations and interviews. *Journal of Criminal Justice*, 33(3), 225–238.

Schanzenbach, M. (2005). Have federal judges changed their sentencing practices? The shaky empirical foundations of the Feener Amendment. *Journal of Empirical Legal Studies*, 2(1), 1–48.

Schwartz-Soicher, O., Geller, A., & Garfinkel, I. (2011). The effect of paternal incarceration on maternal hardship. *Social Service Review*, 85(3), 447–473.

Scully, D., & Marolla, J. (1985). Convicted rapists' vocabulary of motive: Excuses and motivations. *Social Problems*, 31(5), 530–544.

Senior, O. (1991). *Working Miracles: Women's Lives in the English-Speaking Caribbean*. Barbados: ISER.

Sharma, S. (2010, October 20). India tops in shoplifting, losses near Rs10,000. *Daily News and Analysis*.

Sharpe, J. (1996). Mental health issues and family socialization in the Caribbean. In J. Roopnarine, & J. Brown (Ed.), *Caribbean Families: Diversity Among Ethnic Groups* (pp. 205–222). Greenwich, CT: Ablex.

Shepherd, V. (1999). *Women in Caribbean History*. Kingston: Ian Randle.

Sigle-Rushton, W., & Lindstrom, E. (2013). Intersectionality. In M. Evans, & C. Williams (Eds.), *Gender: Key Concepts* (pp. 129–135). London: Routledge.

Simon, H. (1976). *Administrative Behaviour* (3rd Ed.). New York: The Free Press.

Simon, H. (1997). *An Empirically Based Macroeconomics*. Cambridge: Cambridge University Press.

Simon, R. (1975). *Women and Crime.* Lexington, KY: Heath and Company.

Simon, R., & Ahn-Redding, H. (2005). *The Crimes Women Commit.* Oxford: Lexington Books.

Simpson, S., & Elis, L. (1995). Doing gender: Sorting out the caste and crime conundrum. *Criminology,* 33(1), 47–81.

Smith, R. (1996). *The Matrifocal Family: Power, Pluralism and Politics.* New York: Routledge.

Soares, J. (2012). Women on trial: Towards a just criminal justice system. Occassional Paper Series.

Spohn, C., & Belchner, D. (2000). Is preferential treatment of felony offenders a thing of the past? A miltisite study of gender, race and imprisonment. *Criminal Justice Policy Review,* 11, 149–184.

Spohn, D., Beichner, D., & Davis-Frenzel, E. (2001). Prosecutorial justifications for sexual assault case rejections: Guarding the "gateway to justice". *Social Problems,* 48, 206–235.

Sroufe, L., & Causadias, J. (2012). *Maternal Incarceration, Separation and Child Development: Evidence and Alternatives.* Santiago de Chile: United Nations Children's Fund.

Steffensmeier, D. (1980a). Assessing the impact of the women's movement on sex-based differences in the handling of adult criminal defendents. *Crime and Delinquency,* 26, 344–357.

Steffensmeier, D. (1980b). Sex differences in patterns of adult crime 1965–1977: A review and assessment. *Social Forces,* 58, 1080–1108.

Steffensmeier, D., & Allan, E. (1996). Gender and Crime: Toward a genedered theory of female offending. *Annual Review of Sociology,* 22, 459–487.

Steffensmeier, D., & Demuth, S. (2006). Does gender modify the effects of race-ethnicity on criminal sanctions? Sentences for male and female, white, black and hispanic defendants. *Journal of Quantitative Criminology,* 22, 241–261.

Steffensmeier, D., & Montivans, M. (2000). Older men and older women in the arms of criminal law: Offending patterns and sentencing outcomes. *Journal of Gerontology,* 55(3), 141–151.

Steffensmeier, D., Kramer, J., & Streifel, C. (1993). Gender and imprisonment decisions. *Criminology,* 31, 441–446.

Stolzenberg, L., & D'Alessio, S. (2004). Sex differences in the likelihood of arrest. *Journal of Criminal Justice,* 32, 443–454.

Sugie, N. (2012). Punishment and welfare: Paternal incarceration and families' receipt of public assistance. *Social Forces,* 90(4), 1403–1427.

Sundberg, J. (2004). Identitites in the making: Conservation, gender adn race in the Maya Biosphere Reserve, Guatamala. *Gender, Place and Culture,* 11(1), 43–66.

Sutherland, E. (1939). *Principles of Criminology.* Philadelphia: J. B. Lippincott.

Sutton, H., & Ruprah, I. (2017). *Restoring Paradise in the Caribbean: Combatting Violence with Numbers.* Washingtion, DC: Inter-American Development Bank.

The Crime Report. (2018). Crime cartels revive Caribbean cocaine pipeline. Retrieved November 2019, from *The Crime Report: Your Criminal Justice Network*: https://thecrimereport.org/2018/05/25/crime-cartels-revive-caribbean-cocaine-pipeline/

Thomas, W. (1923). *The Unadjusted Girl*. Boston, MA: Little, Brown.

Ulmer, J. (1997). *Social Worlds of Sentencing: Court Communities Under Sentending Guidelines*. Albany: State University of New York Press.

Ulmer, J., & Johnson, B. (2004). Sentencing context: A multilevel analysis. *Criminology*, 42, 137–177.

UNDP. (2016). *Human Developemnt Report 2016: Human Development for Everyone*. New York: United Nations Development Programme.

UNICEF. (2002). *Multiple Indicator Cluster Survey*. Trinidad and Tobago. New York: UNICEF.

United States v. Booker, U.S. (220 2005).

UNODC. (2013). *Global Study on Homicide: Trends, Context, Data*. United Nations Office on Drugs and Crime. Vienna: UNODC.

UNODC; World Bank. (2007). *Crime, Violence and Development: Trends Costs and Policy Options in the Caribbean*. Washington, DC: World Bank.

USSC. (1987). *United States Sentencing Commission Guidelines Manual*. Washington, DC: United States Sentencing Commission.

USSC. (2004). *Fifteen Years of Guideline Sentencing: An Assessment of How Well the Federal Justice System Is Acheiving the Goals of Sentencing Reform*. Washington, DC: United States Sentencing Commission.

Verma Singh, A. (2016). The influence of patriarchy on gender roles. *International Journal of English Language, Literature, and Translation Studies*, 3(1), 27–29.

Visher, C. (1983). Gender, police arrest decisions, and notions of chivalry. *Criminology*, 20(1), 5–28.

Wakefield, S., & Wildeman, C. (2018). How parental incarceration harms children and what to do about it. National Council on Family Relations. *Policy Brief*, 3(1), 1–6.

Walby, S. (1990). *Theorizing Patriarchy*. Oxford: Basil Blackwell.

Wallace, R., Fullilove, M., & Flisher, A. (1996). AIDS, violence and behavioural coding: Information theory, risk behaviour, and dynamic prcess on core-group sociogeogrpahic networks. *Social Science and Medicine*, 43(3), 339–352.

Walmsley, R. (2017). World Female Imprisonment List: Women and girls in penal institutions, including pre-trial detainees/remand prisoners. Retrieved January 3, 2020, from prisonstudies.org: www.prisonstudies.org/sites/default/files/resources/downloads/world_female_prison_4th_edn_v4_web.pdf

Warr, P., Banks, M., & Ullah, P. (1985). The experience of unemployment among black and white urban teenagers. *British Journal of Psychology*, 76, 75–87.

Weisbrot, M. (2011, July 22). Jamaica remains buried under a mountain of debt despite restructuring. *The Guardian*.

West, C., & Zimmerman, D. (1987). Doing gender. *Gender and Society*, 1(2), 125–151.

Widom, C. (2000). Childhood victimization and the derailment of girls and women to the criminal justice system. In *Research on Women and Girls in the Justice System* (Vol. 3, pp. 27–36). Washington, DC: NIJ Research Foum.

Wiemann, G., & Fishman, G. (1988). Attribution of responsibility: Sex-based bias in press reports on crime. *European Journal of Communication*, 3, 415–430.

Wikstrom, P. O., Treiber, K., & Hardie, B. (2012). Breaking rules: The social and situational dynamics of young people's urban crime. In J. McGloin, & C. Sullivan (Eds.), *When Crime Appears: The Role of Emergence*. Oxford: Oxford University Press.

Wilczynski, A. (1997). *Child Homicide*. London: Greenwhich Medical.

Wilkinson, R. (1996). *Unhealthy Societies: The Afffliction of Inequality*. London: Routledge.

Wilson, T., Lindsey, S., & Schooler, T. (2000). A model of dual attitudes. *Psychological Review*, 107(1), 101–126.

Winlow, S. (2001). *Badfellas: Crime, Tradition and New Masculinities*. Oxford: Berg.

World Bank. (2001). *Poverty Reduction Strategy Sourcebook*. Washington, DC: World Bank.

World Bank. (2006). *World Development Report 2006: Equity and Development*. Washington, DC: World Bank.

Young, J. (1999). *The Exclusive Society*. London: MacMillan.

Index

Note: **Bold** page numbers refer to tables; *italic* page numbers refer to figures and page numbers followed by "n" denote endnotes.